The News&Observer

TAR HEEL TRIUMPH

NORTH CAROLINA'S UNFORGETTABLE 2017 CHAMPIONSHIP SEASON

This book is available in quantity at special discounts for your group or organization.
For further information, contact:

Triumph Books LLC
814 North Franklin Street
Chicago, Illinois 60610
Phone: (312) 337-0747
www.triumphbooks.com

Printed in U.S.A.
ISBN: 978-1-62937-305-8

The News & Observer
Publisher: Sara Glines
Editor: John Drescher
Book editors: Steve Ruinsky, Scott Sharpe
Writers: Andrew Carter, Luke DeCock
Photographers: Robert Willett, Ethan Hyman, Chuck Liddy
Stories are from *The News & Observer*

Content packaged by Mojo Media, Inc.
Jason Hinman: Creative Director
Joe Funk: Editor

Front and back cover photos by Ethan Hyman - ehyman@newsobserver.com

Ethan Hyman - ehyman@newsobserver.com

CONTENTS

INTRODUCTION

By Luke DeCock

North Carolina's players had just finished the Cooper Test, two miles in 12 minutes, a preseason ritual. And they came together at Roy Williams' house on that August evening, and his wife Wanda had dessert for them as they gathered in the living room, and the coach told that group of players the same thing he had told his team the year before.

"I thought I had in front of me the kind of guys that could win a national championship," Williams said.

He had been wrong in 2016, but only by 4.7 seconds. He was right in 2017. North Carolina's run to a national title may have started there, in that room, when this group was infused with the same confidence their predecessors had slowly built and developed over the course of a season. And this group was able to finish the job, defeating Gonzaga in Glendale for North Carolina's sixth NCAA title.

Even without last year's stars, Marcus Paige and Brice Johnson, the Tar Heels had an enviable collection of talent: the slinky shooting of Justin Jackson and the gritty drive of Joel Berry and the lanky unpredictability of Theo Pinson and the raw athleticism of Isaiah Hicks and the stout dependability of Kennedy Meeks. It was a group that had come to North Carolina despite the NCAA investigation looming overhead and stuck it out, together, to see this to the end.

It was a team with experience, and ability, but there were certainly teams with more of the latter and teams with as much of both. Like Gonzaga. And others. What distinguished North Carolina from the others was the memory of what happened last year, which propelled and motivated the Tar Heels back to a position where they could obtain a second chance.

North Carolina's journey to the national title in 2017 started in 2016, when the Tar Heels were denied by one of the most famous buzzer-beaters in Final Four history.

In the hours after North Carolina lost to Villanova, Meeks was among a handful of players who roamed Houston in an Uber, desperately trying to find something to eat, unable to process what had just happened. The Tar Heels' journey back to the Final Four began then, on that night, with the pain in their hearts fresh. It would fade, but never go away, not until this championship was secured. And then, for these players if not Paige and Johnson, it went away forever.

* * *

Over the summer, Jackson titled the team's group chat "redemption," as clear a statement of what this team intended to do as anything. Still, when did the Tar Heels come to believe this could happen? The realization that this team could be as good as the last one came to different players at different times.

Some, like Berry and Meeks, always believed. Nate Britt and Hicks marveled at how dominant North Carolina was in Hawaii, at the Maui Invitational, and saw the path forward smoothed. When the Tar Heels

Kennedy Meeks laughs as Roy Williams puts the net over the head of Isaiah Hicks. Meeks and Hicks were instrumental in the dominant frontcourt performance that helped UNC win the championship game. (Ethan Hyman - ehyman@newsobserver.com)

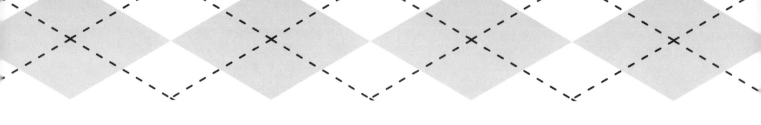

survived a tough ACC swing, hosting Florida State and Syracuse in a three-day span, Pinson could sense the team thriving under NCAA tournament conditions. And the Senior Night victory over Duke, a team that came into the season the national-title favorite, convinced Luke Maye that there was no one North Carolina could not beat.

The Tar Heels were able to match the feat of their predecessors in winning the ACC regular-season title, but Duke in Brooklyn denied them a second ACC championship. That was the final stumble for North Carolina, not that the path to Glendale was a straight line — most notably because Berry sprained his right ankle in the opener, then the left in the regional final against Kentucky, tapping so many bad memories of injured North Carolina point guards.

In Greenville, S.C. — instead of Greensboro, thanks to House Bill 2 — North Carolina let a 17-point lead over Arkansas fizzle away to nothing, and even fell behind by five with three minutes to play. The Tar Heels were forced to confront the reality that their season could end in the second round, at which point Hicks, the quiet senior from Oxford, spoke up: "It can't end like this. We just gotta do something."

With frenetic defense and timely offense, North Carolina scored the game's final 12 points — the kind of gritty victory the Tar Heels had yet to connive over the course of the season. They would wait only a week to draw upon that experience, down five to Kentucky — a far more fearsome and powerful opponent — with five minutes to play in the regional final.

Two nights earlier, Maye had exploded for 16 points and 12 rebounds, an instant hero in a win over Butler, the sophomore who started out a walk-on, son of a former UNC quarterback, now a national story. He was just getting started.

North Carolina was able to erase the five-point deficit and take a seven-point lead with another 12-0 run, but Kentucky's Malik Monk hit a sideways-sliding 3-pointer to tie the score with 7.2 seconds to play, the functional equivalent of Paige's double-clutch 3-pointer to tie the score against Villanova. And Maye, the Most

Outstanding Player of the South Regional, was left open trailing the play to receive a pass from Pinson and send the Tar Heels back to the Final Four.

* * *

As important as the Villanova game was to positioning the Tar Heels for the season they had, the Arkansas game had as much of an impact on their progress through the tournament. Against Kentucky, they drew upon that experience and produced an identical 12-0 run to turn the game around, even if they still needed Maye's unexpected heroics to finish it. And again, against Oregon, the Tar Heels would think back to Arkansas, when they faced premature defeat.

The Tar Heels were in firm control against the Ducks with five minutes to play but did not make a shot the rest of the way. The lead shrank and shrank, until it was whittled all the way down to one in the final seconds. Meeks went to the line and missed two free throws with 5.8 seconds to go, only for Pinson to tip the rebound out to Berry. But Berry missed both of his free throws, only for Meeks to claim the rebound and throw it to Pinson, who dribbled out the clock and hurled the ball into the air.

Once again, the Tar Heels saved their season — and nothing less than a chance to play for the national title would ever have sufficed. Redemption, long sought, was finally at hand.

And so this team shunted aside history, doing something its predecessors could not. No one will ever forget what happened last year, but they'll remember it now only in the context of how it led to this, how this group of players wrote their own chapter in North Carolina history, adding this season to 1957 and 1982 and 1993 and 2005 and 2009 — and giving Williams his third national title in 14 years at his alma mater.

There wasn't a Michael Jordan or Tyler Hansbrough on this team, only a group of players who became more than the sum of their parts, who stuck together, year after year, under some adverse circumstances both within and outside of their control, who found redemption in the end. ■

Roy Williams goes up to cut down the championship net for the third time in his illustrious tenure with the Tar Heels. (Chuck Liddy - cliddy@newsobserver.com)

NCAA TOURNAMENT TITLE GAME
APRIL 3, 2017 · GLENDALE, ARIZONA
NORTH CAROLINA 71, GONZAGA 65

HEARTBREAK TO HAPPINESS

UNC Survives, Earns Sixth NCAA Tournament Championship

By Andrew Carter

Back on the East Coast it was near midnight, near the one-year anniversary, to the day, of North Carolina's greatest heartbreak — one that united this team on a long-sought mission of redemption. It was near midnight there when the Tar Heels began celebrating here.

For the past year, they'd often spoken of their hope of reaching this point, the final Monday night of the college basketball season. Roy Williams, the UNC coach, had often spoken with tears in his eyes about how last season ended. Like so many times before during this long postseason run — like against Arkansas in the second round, and against Kentucky in the South Regional semifinal, and against Oregon here on Saturday night in a national semifinal — UNC survived. Imperiled late in all those victories, it survived.

"Our guys, I told them with three minutes to play — if you'd have told us the first day of practice that we would be in the championship game with that score with three minutes to play, everybody would have taken it," Williams said. "But we had to play the last three minutes."

At the media timeout with about three minutes remaining, UNC led 62-60. A minute later, though, the Tar Heels found themselves in the same position they were in against Arkansas, and against Kentucky and Oregon, too: needing to be nearly perfect in a game's most dramatic moments.

Gonzaga, the upstart mid-major major that was attempting to break through with its first national championship led by two points after Nigel Williams-Goss' jumper from near the top of the key. As it turned out, that was the final time the Bulldogs scored.

UNC, so calm in these situations throughout the tournament, was at its best in the final minutes. It closed the game on an 8-0 run, taking the lead for good on Justin Jackson's three-point play with one minute, 40 seconds remaining.

A little more than a minute later, after a defensive stop, Isaiah Hicks, the senior forward, gave the Tar Heels a 68-65 lead with 22 seconds remaining. It was Hicks who blamed himself after UNC's 77-74 loss against Villanova in the national championship game a season ago.

He was the closest player, after all, to Kris Jenkins, who made the winning 3-pointer as time expired, sending confetti raining down while UNC walked slowly off the court. Hicks had labored through UNC's past four games, failing to score in double figures in any of them.

Isaiah Hicks lays in two late in the second half during UNC's dramatic victory over Gonzaga. Hicks overcame poor shooting throughout the NCAA Tournament to finish with an indispensable 13 points and nine rebounds. (Ethan Hyman - ehyman@newsobserver.com)

On Monday night his running one-hander as the shot clock ran out, the one with 22 seconds remaining on the game clock, might have been the game's most important shot. Afterward Hicks wore one of the championship nets around his neck.

"I was trying," he said. "That's all I can do, is try and leave everything out here."

This time it was the Tar Heels' turn to savor the ending. And this time Hicks, who finished with 13 points and nine rebounds while hampered by foul trouble, earned some measure of redemption.

All of his teammates did, too, as did Williams, even if he wasn't necessarily seeking it. He said the defeat last season didn't keep him up at night, that he didn't dwell on it. But he allowed it to fuel him, as did his players.

"It does," Williams said, asked if this helped soothe what happened a year ago. "But I was killed last year, and this doesn't make me go back and feel better about last year. I just feel for Marcus Paige and Brice Johnson, Joel James, that they didn't get to experience the feeling that our kids now are feeling."

Williams said he wrote a message to his team up on the white board inside the team's locker room. It was a message about the necessity of toughness. No one personified that characteristic more than Joel Berry II, the junior point guard who earned Final Four Most Outstanding Player honors.

Hobbled by two injured ankles throughout the NCAA tournament, Berry finished with 22 points. He made four 3-pointers. He had the assist, after Kennedy Meeks' blocked shot, that led to Justin Jackson's game-sealing, breakaway dunk with 12 seconds remaining.

"I wanted to yell as loud as I possibly could," Jackson, who finished with 16 points, said of that play. "But I had nothing in me. And coach was yelling at me to get back, and the tears started rolling. I mean, it was a whole bunch of different emotions."

This wasn't a game that will be remembered for its artistic beauty. Both Williams and Mark Few, the Gonzaga coach, praised the effort of their teams. They didn't

Kennedy Meeks delivers the most memorable block of his storied Tar Heels career, rejecting Gonzaga's Nigel Williams-Goss with 16 seconds remaining in the game. (Ethan Hyman - ehyman@newsobserver.com)

necessarily admire the execution — at least not offensively.

The pace of the game dragged, too, amid a torrent of whistles. The teams combined for 44 fouls — 22 on each team — and neither Gonzaga nor UNC shot better than 36 percent from the field. This was a game that was expected to be decided on the interior, with some of the best post players in the country.

Most all of them, though, found themselves on the bench for long stretches of the second half. UNC's Kennedy Meeks and Hicks both finished with four fouls. Gonzaga's Zach Collins, the 7-foot freshman, fouled out. His teammates Przemek Karnowski — who at 7-foot-1 and 300 pounds resembles a bearded brick wall — and Jonathan Williams both finished with three fouls.

An exercise in artistry on offense this was not. And it wasn't so much decided in the paint as it was by UNC's

Opposite: Justin Jackson puts an exclamation point on the win with a resounding breakaway dunk in the closing seconds. Jackson finished with 16 points in the title game. Above: Kennedy Meeks cuts down the net. The senior big man continued his dominance on the glass, grabbing 10 boards in the victory. (Chuck Liddy - cliddy@newsobserver.com)

grit, again, in the final minutes. The Tar Heels didn't allow a point during the final one minute, 53 seconds. Jackson's dunk in the final seconds gave UNC a 70-65 lead.

The Tar Heels could feel it then. Moments later a Gonzaga turnover all but sealed it.

Eight seconds later it was over. Berry and his teammates ran around the court, finding someone to hug. The confetti eventually fell, after an extended delay. The Tar Heels gathered on a stage and hoisted the national championship trophy. They cut down the nets. They watched One Shining Moment.

Nobody could really find the words to describe it. They'd achieved the redemption they'd long sought. ▨

Opposite: Surrounded by his teammates, junior forward Theo Pinson (1) holds up the championship trophy. Pinson had six points and nine rebounds in the unforgettable win. (Ethan Hyman - ehyman@newsobserver.com) Above: Joel Berry II waves to the crowd after cutting off his portion of the net. Berry gave a performance for the ages, earning the Final Four Most Outstanding Player honors. (Chuck Liddy - cliddy@newsobserver.com)

TOL 0 65 ●● BONUS POSS 2ND Half

Justin Jackson (44), Isaiah Hicks (4) and Joel Berry II (2) celebrate during the waning seconds in the Tar Heels' redemptive championship triumph. (Ethan Hyman - ehyman@newsobserver.com)

MISSION ACCOMPLISHED

One Year After Devastating Loss, Tar Heels Write Storybook Ending

By Luke DeCock

It just so happened all five starters touched the ball in the final seconds, Isaiah Hicks with the biggest basket of his career on the final basket of his career, Kennedy Meeks blocking a shot, Joel Berry throwing the ball ahead to Justin Jackson for a dunk, Theo Pinson hurling the ball into the air as time expired.

It was like everyone had to get a piece of it, the redemption they sought for so long, finally at hand. North Carolina would not be denied this time, not by a buzzer-beater, not by anyone.

This group, this uncommon group of veteran players in an era of one-and-dones and transfers, took its place in not only North Carolina history but basketball history, losing the title game one year — in the most heartbreaking fashion imaginable — only to come back a year later and finish the job.

They can now take credit for the Smith Center's sixth NCAA banner — the third under Roy Williams in 14 years at North Carolina — after Monday's 71-65 win over Gonzaga, the fulfillment finally washing away last year's frustration.

"That's cool," Jackson said. "I think that's a storybook ending to a journey we've had from last year until now. That's unbelievable, and I can't reiterate it enough and say how proud I am of everyone in this locker room."

Of course, it wasn't easy. It never was for this team in this tournament. If anything, it was a testament to how talented the Tar Heels truly were that they were able to win the title at something less than full speed, game after game.

In a choppy, whistle-happy game that saw every big man for both teams in foul trouble, North Carolina finally took control in the final 100 seconds. With 26 seconds to go and the Tar Heels up one, Hicks made the biggest shot of his career, a leaner in the lane despite all his struggles during the tournament. Meeks blocked Nigel Williams-Goss, the ball fell to Berry and he threw the ball the length of the court to Jackson for a dunk.

At that moment, the Tar Heels knew they had won, that they were 12 seconds away from a victory that would come after a Berry free throw, Pinson hurling the ball high into the air as time expired.

The Tar Heels never once in the tournament had all their parts clicking at once, and that was true Monday as well. Berry was back, finally looking free of the ankle issues that plagued him throughout the tournament, and Hicks finally had a few shots drop. But Jackson and Pinson struggled mightily, and Meeks was resolute defensively against Gonzaga's gargantuan Przemek Karnowski and other bigs but couldn't get anything going on offense.

And still, for all that, they join the great teams in North Carolina history, the sixth to win an NCAA title, the second championship by an ACC team in three years.

"All the former guys were saying, just pull up a chair

Theo Pinson (1), Justin Jackson (44) and Joel Berry II (2) are elated, as the buzzer sounds and they've officially clinched the sixth national championship in North Carolina's incredible history. (Ethan Hyman - ehyman@newsobserver.com)

at the table," Pinson said. "We wanted to pull up a chair. I told Sean (May) after the game, clean my chair off and have it ready when we come up to the table."

Win or lose against Gonzaga, the mere fact that the Tar Heels were able to make it back to the national championship game was a significant accomplishment of its own. Only eight teams have lost the title one year and come back to play for it the next.

This wasn't easy, even if it looks like it now. Not only was this where the bar was set for this season — anything less than this would have been perceived, internally and externally, as failure, whether that's fair or not — but the Tar Heels were thinking about this the entire time.

The odds against making it back to this point were astronomical, and the Tar Heels could have stumbled at any point along the way. At times — against Arkansas, against Kentucky, especially right down to the end against Oregon — it seemed like they were even trying to shake off the fate they felt they deserved, only to regroup and continue to march forward toward it.

"Last year happened for a reason. We got a second chance," Hicks said. "It's all about taking advantage of that. It doesn't come often you're in back-to-back national championship games. So why not win this one?"

Even though Monday wasn't North Carolina's best game, they would not be denied. This team had an uncommon mission, a shared purpose. The title wrested from their hands once, they claimed it at the end, all five starters touching the ball in victory, in success, in destiny. ■

SURVIVE AND ADVANCE

Tar Heels Barely Hold Off Oregon, Fight Their Way Back Into Final

By Andrew Carter

During the final 5.8 seconds on Saturday night, North Carolina clinging to a one-point lead against Oregon in an NCAA tournament national semifinal, Kennedy Meeks was talking to himself and Joel Berry was thinking he couldn't miss and Theo Pinson was stunned, bewildered.

"Can we make one?" Pinson said he was thinking, again and again, while one missed free throw turned into two misses, and then three, and then four, when Berry's second attempt bounced off the left side of the rim with four seconds remaining.

At that moment, the Tar Heels had missed four consecutive free throws in the final six seconds. They had kept alive Oregon's hope of completing a stunning comeback. Something that seemed unfathomable minutes earlier appeared possible: UNC's season could again end in anguish and agony for the second consecutive year.

It might have, too, if not for two offensive rebounds in the final 5.8 seconds. Pinson secured the first, after Meeks missed the second of his two free throws. Meeks secured the second, after Berry missed the second of his two free throws. And then the ball wound up in Pinson's hands.

He dribbled it five times and then threw it high above the court inside the cavernous University of Phoenix Stadium. The Tar Heels prevailed — a 77-76 victory that sends them into the national championship game for the 11th time in school history.

UNC, the top seed in the South Region, will play against Gonzaga, the top seed in the West. The Tar Heels, so driven by a season-long quest of redemption, are back in the national championship game for the second consecutive year.

Everyone remembers how the last one ended: Marcus Paige's improbable shot with 4.7 seconds remaining to tie Villanova at 74. And then Kris Jenkins' 3-pointer to win it at the buzzer, sending the Tar Heels back to their locker room, heartbroken, while the confetti streamed down.

More than one UNC player thought about that moment on Saturday night. The Tar Heels led by 10 points with 8½ minutes remaining. And then, inexplicably, their offense sputtered and they began missing shots, and they began playing with passiveness, instead of aggression.

"And we didn't do a good job of just continuing to attack them," Berry said. "We did a horrible job of that."

And then it was a one-point game in the final seconds, the Tar Heels unable to make a shot from the

North Carolina's Joel Berry II drives to the basket while teammate Luke Maye (32) contends with Oregon defenders. (Robert Willett - rwillett@newsobserver.com)

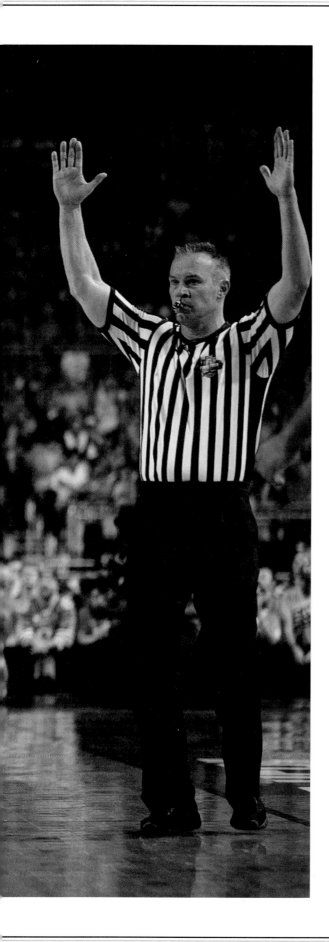

field, and unable to make one from the free throw line, either. All Oregon needed was a possession to either tie or take the lead.

UNC has been the best offensive rebounding team in college basketball this season. The Tar Heels lead the nation in offensive rebounding percentage, and their ability to secure misses was never more important than it was in the final seconds on Saturday night, a national championship game appearance at stake.

First came the free throws that Meeks missed. He played brilliantly otherwise — 25 points and 14 rebounds, and it was arguably his best game in his four seasons at UNC. He stepped to the free throw line with 5.8 seconds remaining with a chance to set a career scoring high.

"I work so hard every practice to make as many free throws I can before we leave," he said.

His first attempt, though, was short, off the front rim, and in that moment Pinson's instincts told him that it could happen again — that Meeks could be short. Pinson knew that, he said, because usually it's easier for a shooter to correct a free throw that sails too long than one that doesn't go far enough.

And so Meeks released his second attempt. Short again.

"I guess he didn't think I was going to go for it," Pinson said of Jordan Bell, the Oregon forward who was helpless to stop Pinson from getting his hand on Meeks' second miss. "And I just got a firm hand on it, I just threw it right to Joel. It was sort of a tip-out, but it was literally a throw to him."

Now UNC had life again: possession and a one-point lead with the clock running. Oregon immediately fouled, sending Berry to the line.

Entering Saturday night Berry had made 80.8 percent of his free throws. Nobody on the team had made a greater percentage. If UNC could have chosen anybody to step to the free throw line in the final seconds of a close game, it'd have been Berry.

And now here he was. If he'd made both, Oregon would have needed to make a 3-pointer to send the game to overtime.

Justin Jackson is ecstatic after sinking a 3-pointer for a 46-38 second-half lead. North Carolina held a much slimmer margin of victory in the end, beating Oregon 77-76 to earn a spot in the finals. (Robert Willett - rwillett@newsobserver.com)

"Joel, our best free throw shooter comes up — all right, that's an automatic two," said Justin Jackson, the junior forward who scored 13 of his 22 points in the second half.

This time, it was not an automatic two. Berry's first attempt bounced off to the right. His second bounced off to the left. All the while, those cheering for UNC here stood in a stunned, ominous silence. Some put their hands on their heads. They stood in dreadful anticipation of what might go wrong next.

The Tar Heels practice for these moments, though. They practice for these moments often, Meeks said, though it's difficult to practice free throw rebounding — or any rebounding, for that matter — given the unpredictability of the bounces.

Nonetheless, UNC coach Roy Williams tells his players all the time: The only person who should expect a free throw to go in is the one attempting it. Everyone else should be expecting a miss, and preparing to rebound.

And so that's what Meeks was thinking before Berry released his second attempt: Meeks was thinking that it'd miss, and he was preparing to position himself. He was next to Bell, the Oregon forward who allowed Pinson the rebound after Meeks' miss, and Meeks earlier had made a point to remember one of Bell's tendencies.

"I saw him bite a couple of times early on the other free throws," Meeks said. "So I just tried to bury him. Coach always says, 'expect a miss,' so I did. And the ball fell in my hand."

And then it was out of his hands, back to Pinson outside the top of the key. He took five dribbles.

He threw the ball high into the air after the horn sounded. The Tar Heels, who didn't make a shot from the field in a span of nearly six minutes at the end, were off to the national championship game. The Tar Heels, who nearly surrendered a 10-point lead with 8½ minutes to play, advanced to the final Monday night for the second consecutive season.

More than once late on Saturday night, Williams spoke of luck. He spoke of his team's good fortune.

North Carolina's Theo Pinson (1) knocks the rebound from Oregon's Jordan Bell (1) after a missed free throw by UNC's Kennedy Meeks (3) late in the second half. The Tar Heels' rebounding ability proved crucial amid uncharacteristic free throw misses late in the game. (Ethan Hyman - ehyman@newsobserver.com)

"But that's okay," Williams said of those things. "Doesn't make any difference — we're still one of the two teams playing on Monday night."

This was the kind of victory that can cause coaches to age beyond their years. Pinson, though, believed that Williams would look back on the ending with fondness, and that he might draw on it the way Williams draws on so much other history with his current group of players.

In years to come, Williams might well find himself describing what UNC experienced on Saturday: a dwindling lead, the pressure mounting, the shots clanking off the rim, one after the other. Williams might find himself describing four missed free throws, and the will and skill to secure two of those misses.

"I think coach will definitely, when we're gone, will tell that story," Pinson said. "Because that just shows how big offensive rebounding is — boxing out at the end of the game. And I'm sure they wish they boxed out right there."

Oregon wished it had. Several Oregon players crumpled to the floor when it ended. All the Ducks needed was one final possession, one final shot. Given the sequence of events in the final minutes, the odds appeared in the Ducks' favor. They received the help they needed in the form of UNC's missed free throws.

But the Tar Heels secured those misses. First Pinson. And then Meeks, who passed out to Pinson.

"Exhilarating," Jackson said, asked to describe the final moments in a word. "We'll say exhilarating."

He described the misses, the rebounds, Meeks grabbing the game's final miss — UNC's final offensive rebound against the shorter Ducks. It was the most important play of what was likely Meeks' best game, and then the Tar Heels were off to the final Monday night, back again in the national championship game. ■

Kennedy Meeks (3) secures an offensive rebound with less than four seconds to play. Meeks' 25 points and 14 rebounds were an essential ingredient in North Carolina's Final Four win. (Robert Willett - rwillett@newsobserver.com)

TO HAVE AND HAVE NOT

On the Heels of Notable Departures, UNC Looks Toward Newer Stars

By Luke DeCock • October 11, 2016

On what is essentially the first public day of a new basketball season, there was an awful lot of talk about the two guys we know for certain will not play for North Carolina this year.

Marcus Paige and Brice Johnson are gone, but their considerable absence hung over the Tar Heels' media day like the banners honoring them will one day hang over the Smith Center court. Most of the questions asked Tuesday were about how they will be replaced, on the court, in the locker room, in every way.

"Those other guys, as I've said many times, and will say many times again, really need to step up," North Carolina coach Roy Williams said. "Because it's not two out of eight. It's your two best. Markedly, maybe you could say your two best in every part of the game. It's not just a numbers game."

Williams, to use the kind of golf analogy he delights in, is sandbagging a little. He might not have Paige and Johnson, but he has all the tools he needs. It's probably foolish to say that this team can be as good or better than its predecessor, which was a shot or two away from winning a national title, but there's no reason it can't come close.

Duke harbors legitimate Final Four hopes, but it isn't the only team in the Triangle that does. And

because North Carolina lost such high-profile players, it's easy to overlook the talent the Tar Heels do have. There are six McDonald's All-Americans on this roster, the MVP of the ACC tournament (Joel Berry), a consistent double-digit scorer capable of much more (Justin Jackson), the experience of Nate Britt and Kennedy Meeks and the as-yet-unharnessed talent and athleticism of Theo Pinson and Isaiah Hicks.

Any of those six would claim a starting spot on just about any ACC roster. Throw in freshman big man Tony Bradley and shooter Kenny Williams, little used as a freshman, as well as reserves Luke Maye and Stilman White, and there may not be as much talent and depth here as there was a year ago, but there's plenty. This group just lacks the resume of its illustrious predecessors.

"We understand we haven't done anything yet as a team," Pinson said. "We have to go out there and prove what we can do as a team, and we're going to go out there and try and do that."

There is unquestionably a changing of the guard for the Tar Heels, one that started to gain traction a year ago when Paige and Johnson were still around, with Berry's emergence as a go-to player and Pinson's development over the course of the season. Because of

North Carolina's Justin Jackson, Kennedy Meeks and Joel Berry II pose together during the Tar Heels' media day, ahead of the 2016-2017 season. All three players took on greater roles for UNC following the graduations of Marcus Paige and Brice Johnson. (Robert Willett - rwillett@newsobserver.com)

the relative dearth of big men, the Tar Heels may even be more inclined to go small with Pinson or Jackson at the 4, a strategy that produced some of North Carolina's best moments a year ago.

That junior class of Berry and Pinson and Jackson is the key for North Carolina; the Tar Heels will go as far as those players can take them.

"We've always said our time is coming," Berry said. "We've always felt like this year is the year — we have seniors, but the core people on this team are probably us, because we're the most experienced. It's something we think about all the time, that this year is our year to be able to do that."

The Tar Heels certainly have something to prove, but it's less about how much they'll miss Paige and Johnson than it is how far they can go with what they have. And as hard as it is to forget about the players they lost, it's just as easy to overlook the players they do have. ■

UNC power forward Kennedy Meeks (3) shoots against N.C. State defenders at PNC Arena in Raleigh. (Ethan Hyman - ehyman@newsobserver.com) Above: North Carolina's Justin Jackson looks to head coach Roy Williams for instruction during a timeout. (Robert Willett - rwillett@newsobserver.com)

DECEMBER 17, 2016 · LAS VEGAS, NEVADA
KENTUCKY 103, NORTH CAROLINA 100

HARMONIOUS MONK

UNC Comes Up Short in Thriller Against UK and Malik Monk
By Andrew Carter

North Carolina this year was already involved in one of the great college basketball games in history, the national championship game more than eight months ago that Villanova won with a 3-pointer at the buzzer.

For a non-conference game in December, though, it's never been better than it was in the CBS Classic between UNC and Kentucky, two bitter non-conference rivals, two of the most storied programs in the history of the sport, the game not decided until the final buzzer.

Again, the Tar Heels were on the other side of history, this after a 103-100 defeat that came in what had to be one of the greatest regular-season games ever played. No one would argue with that assertion, at least, after 40 minutes that had a little bit of everything:

A first half with both teams scoring in the 50s, no shortage of fast breaks, dunks, alley-oops and layups, a dramatic finish with momentum swing after momentum swing. And, oh yes, one of great individual performances, ever, against the Tar Heels.

That came courtesy of Malik Monk, the Kentucky freshman guard. He finished with 47 points, and made shot after shot — after shot — to lift the Wildcats to victory when it seemed in doubt in the final moments.

Only Duke's Dick Groat, who finished with 48 points against UNC in 1952, had ever scored more

against the Tar Heels. Monk's final points, a 3-pointer from the left wing with 22 seconds remaining, were among the Wildcats' most important, if not the most.

The 3 gave Kentucky the lead after the Wildcats had briefly lost it during the final 90 seconds — first on Justin Jackson's 3-pointer with 97 seconds remaining and then again on Jackson's layup with 47 seconds to play, both moments sending the UNC bench into a celebratory uproar.

After Monk's final 3 — he made eight of those, and was 18-for-28 from the field overall — UNC's Isaiah Hicks missed a turnaround on the other end. That forced the Tar Heels to foul — Joel Berry, back after missing the past two games with a sprained ankle — fouled out in the process — and after De'Aaron Fox made a pair of free throws, the Tar Heels called a timeout with 1.4 seconds left.

Their first last-second play ended with Isaiah Briscoe intercepting the in-bounds pass, sliding out of bounds. There was still seven-tenths of a second remaining. Kenny Williams, the sophomore guard, wound up with a good look from the corner, but his shot landed stuck between the rim and the backboard.

And so it ended, a victory that send Kentucky fans running through the aisles, screaming in jubilation at T-Mobile Arena. When John Calipari, the Kentucky

North Carolina's Justin Jackson shoots against Kentucky during the first half of the CBS Sports Classic in Las Vegas. Although the Tar Heels came up short in the 103-100 contest, they came back to beat the Wildcats in the NCAA Tournament in March. (AP Images)

coach, entered a room just off the court for his postgame press conference he exhaled.

"Whew," he said. "... If you watched that game, if you never liked basketball, you're going to like basketball."

Aside from Monk's stellar performance — the Tar Heels had no one who could guard him, not Williams nor Berry nor anyone else — foul trouble also doomed UNC. Both Kennedy Meeks and Berry fouled out, Meeks with 5½ minutes to play and Berry in the final seconds.

Hicks, meanwhile, finished with four fouls and missed about 10 minutes during the second half after he was called for his fourth with about 17½ minutes remaining. He reentered the game with about 6½ minutes to play, along with Berry, who was called for his fourth two minutes earlier.

Monk's performance overshadowed several others. Jackson finished with 34 points, the most he's ever scored in college, and he nearly did enough to help the Tar Heels overcome a 12-point first-half deficit. Berry in his return finished with 23 points, and made three 3s. ■

Opposite: Kentucky's De'Aaron Fox (0) guards against North Carolina's Joel Berry II at mid-court. Above: UK's Isaac Humphries blocks a shot by UNC's Justin Jackson, right, during the first half. (AP Images)

REGULAR SEASON

JANUARY 8, 2017 · CHAPEL HILL, NORTH CAROLINA
NORTH CAROLINA 107, NORTH CAROLINA STATE 56

SUNDAY BREEZE

UNC Sees Red in Record-Breaking Win Against N.C. State

By Andrew Carter

Justin Jackson said he didn't appreciate what was happening until halftime, after he made a 3-pointer from near the top of the key and ran off to the court while people at the Smith Center stood and cheered one of UNC's greatest first-half performances in the history of the building.

Only then, said Jackson, the Tar Heels' junior wing forward, did he pay attention to the margin, then 33 points wide. The numbers began running together, too, for Joel Berry, the junior point guard. At one point he caught a glimpse of the scoreboard and "I was a little surprised," he said.

On the other side of a room after the Tar Heels' 107-56 victory against N.C. State, Isaiah Hicks, the UNC senior forward, was saying that he, too, had blocked out the score — and UNC's ever-growing margin — until it became impossible to ignore.

"I came out and looked up like, 'Dang,' " Hicks said. "I mean, that's all I could say."

That's just about all anyone could say amid this, the Tar Heels' largest margin of victory in an ACC game in school history. They needed about four minutes to take a 10-point lead, and then it grew to 15 points, to 20, to 30, to 45 and kept climbing.

Nobody saw this sort of thing happening. Not Hicks and his teammates and not UNC coach Roy Williams, who spoke afterward, eight days after a stunning loss at Georgia Tech, of "how things swing so quickly" in this sport.

"I thought since it's UNC going against North Carolina State, I thought it was going to be a little edge on their side, as well," said Berry, who finished with 19 points and five assists. "But we came out and jumped on them."

That was perhaps the most succinct way to put it. The details: UNC pressured N.C. State into committing 10 turnovers during the first 11 minutes and hounded the Wolfpack when it managed to generate attempts from the field. Those, though, often missed, and UNC led by 26 points midway through the first half.

Game over, essentially. This on Sunday was early-season UNC — the team that played so well in November that some wondered, with a straight face, whether these Tar Heels might be even better than the ones who played on the final night of the NCAA tournament early last April. It was a fair question about six weeks ago.

And then came the humbling: the ugly loss at Indiana, the inability to hold on late in a thriller against

Point guard Joel Berry II (2) drives past N.C. State's Dennis Smith Jr. (4) to the basket on the way to a 107-56 victory. Berry put up 19 points in the Tar Heels' dominant showing. (Ethan Hyman - ehyman@newsobserver.com)

Kentucky and then whatever it was that ailed the Tar Heels last weekend in Atlanta, where they lost by 12 points against a Georgia Tech team that was picked to finish 14th in the 15-team ACC.

Amid those defeats were slow starts and closer-than-expected victories, sluggish wins against Davidson, Tennessee and Clemson. And there was another question, too, far different from the one in November: What happened to the team that looked so good on its way to the Maui Invitational championship?

That team returned on Sunday, after a 17-hour wait to get going. That was the length of postponement after UNC's game against N.C. State, originally scheduled for 8 p.m. on Saturday, was moved to early Sunday afternoon. Berry passed the time on Saturday night, he said, watching movies, staying in.

He focused on the task ahead. He'd heard all the talk about N.C. State's Dennis Smith Jr., the freshman who some say might be good enough to be the No. 1 pick in the NBA draft next summer. This wasn't about Berry vs. Smith, Berry said.

Still, said Berry, "I'm a competitive person, and I don't want anyone saying that someone's better than I am. And that's why I had a little edge today, and I always go out there with an edge... I just felt like I wanted the edge on him, and I did that today."

Smith committed two fouls during the first four minutes, while UNC built that early 10-point lead. Then came Smith's third foul midway through the first half. Mark Gottfried, the N.C. State coach, reacted with so much disgust his outburst cost him a technical foul.

About the same time, a small bird flew across the court, creating a momentary diversion. When things continued, with Smith on the bench the rest of the half, it became no less like a twilight zone of dysfunction for the Wolfpack.

N.C. State endured its second-worst defeat in school history — second only to a 52-point defeat against UNC in 1921, at the venerable Bynum Gymnasium on UNC's

North Carolina's Kenny Williams (24) drives to the basket to give the Tar Heels an early 16-4 lead in front of the Smith Center crowd. (Robert Willett - rwillett@newsobserver.com)

campus. The Tar Heels, meanwhile, made history of their own by going back to their recent past.

"Maui was really kind of the last time that we had that fire in us," said Jackson, who led UNC with 21 points.

It continued to burn throughout on Sunday.

The Tar Heels played with a sense of relentlessness, and they didn't settle when they led by 20 points or even 30 or 40. Defensively, UNC maintained its pressure and forced 26 turnovers. The Tar Heels turned those into a season-high 37 points, and afterward Williams and his players said their rout began there, with defense.

UNC's dominance had roots elsewhere, too. It had roots in the return of Theo Pinson, the junior who had five rebounds and five assists in his first game back from a broken foot. It had roots in Berry's personal motivation against Smith, and in Williams' personal disdain for the Wolfpack, an animosity that has lingered for decades.

UNC is now 26-3 against N.C. State since Williams became the Tar Heels' head coach in 2003. Years ago, Berry said he was well-versed in the UNC-Duke basketball rivalry. Since arriving at UNC, Berry had become acquainted with another.

"Once I got here I realized how a lot of people don't really like N.C. State," he said. "And to tell you the truth, I think it's more of a hatred for N.C. State than it is for Duke, in my opinion."

This, then, was a performance especially easy to love for the Tar Heels, who according to the final margin of victory were never more dominant in any ACC game, ever, than they were on Sunday against their bitter old rival. ■

North Carolina's Justin Jackson (44) launches a 3-pointer over N.C. State's Maverick Rowan (24). Jackson hit 6 of 11 from beyond the arc and led all scorers with 21 points in the record-breaking rout. (Robert Willett - rwillett@newsobserver.com)

ELITE 800

After Milestone Win, Roy Williams Remembers His Start

By Andrew Carter • January 17, 2017

Roy Williams had answered questions about Isaiah Hicks and Justin Jackson, had talked about how North Carolina tried to counter Syracuse's zone defense and had tried to describe the moment — winning his 800th game as a head coach. Now he looked past the cameras toward the man in the back of the room.

"Does anybody else got a question?" Williams asked on Monday night, after his team's 85-68 victory against Syracuse, and when no one said anything he went on. "All right, I'll leave it with this — back here is coach Buddy Baldwin. And that was my high school coach.

"And if it wasn't for him, I wouldn't be a coach today."

It had been an emotional scene earlier. When the final seconds expired on the Tar Heels' 17th victory of the season — and their fifth consecutive, after that stunning New Year's Eve defeat at Georgia Tech — a celebration began. Williams had accomplished, with his 800th career victory, what only eight other coaches in NCAA Division I men's college basketball history had ever done.

There was a montage that played high above the court, on the video boards in the upper corners of the Smith Center: Players Williams had coached over the years at Kansas, then at UNC, giving thanks, telling Williams how much they appreciated him. There was Raef LaFrentz, the Kansas forward. And Marcus Paige, who helped lead the Tar Heels to the Final Four a season ago.

There was Milt Newton, who was on Williams' first team at Kansas. Nearly 30 years and 799 victories later, Newton spoke of how proud he was to have been a part of Williams' first victory as a college head coach. The tributes went on. More than once it looked like Williams wiped something away from his eyes. UNC presented him with a commemorative jersey, some souvenir shoes signed by Michael Jordan. Players wore shirts with "800" on them.

Williams turned to his players, the ones who solved the Orange's 2-3 zone and then withstood a couple of Syracuse rallies in the second-half before pulling away late. Hicks finished with 20 points, the first time at UNC he'd ever scored at least 20 in consecutive games. Jackson finished with 19 points and 10 rebounds; Kennedy Meeks with a double-double, too: 15 points and 12 rebounds.

"It was never a dream of mine to win 800 games," Williams said, holding a microphone and addressing his players as much as those who'd remained in their seats. "But it was a dream of mine to coach guys like this."

With his team's 85-68 victory against Syracuse, Roy Williams achieved his historic 800th win as a head coach. (Robert Willett - rwillett@newsobserver.com)

Baldwin, the old high school coach, was standing in front of his seat — first row behind the Syracuse bench. He sits there often, he said, and provides Williams with support, vocal and moral.

Williams played for Baldwin back in the mid-to-late 1960s at T.C. Roberson High in Asheville. Williams had never encountered a man like Baldwin, and Baldwin, 76, perhaps had never encountered a high school kid like Williams.

"Special," is how Baldwin on Monday described this, watching Williams win his 800th game.

"It really was," Baldwin said in a hallway in the Smith Center not far from the Tar Heels locker room. "I've known Roy since 1965, and he is just a special person. I coached him, I loved coaching him. A great competitor. And we have been best of friends for many years. We play golf together, we do a lot of things together.

"And tonight was special for him, and special for me, too."

Williams joked about that later, about his relationship with Baldwin. The way Williams tells it, Baldwin inspired him to become a coach, turned him onto golf and taught him how to shoot craps, too.

"So Wanda thinks he's 0-for-3," Williams said, referring to his wife.

If Williams, who was raised mostly by his mother, hadn't encountered Baldwin in his high school years, he might not have been standing there on the court at the Smith Center in the aftermath of his 800th victory. There might not have even been a first victory, or a life in coaching at all.

Williams, after all, was set to attend Georgia Tech on an engineering scholarship. Yet his time with Baldwin inspired him to consider another path.

"I knew he wanted to be a coach," Baldwin said, "and I thought he was going to Georgia Tech to be an engineer. And I said Roy, if you want to be a coach — I went to school here — I said, 'Go to Carolina. Get with coach (Dean) Smith.' And he came down here, and the rest is history."

By years, Williams became the fastest coach to win 800 games. He reached the milestone in the second-fewest games

Head Coach Roy Williams poses with his players, showing off a commemorative "800" jersey.
(Robert Willett - rwillett@newsobserver.com)

anybody ever has, only behind Adolph Rupp. Afterward somebody asked Williams how he'd changed between victory No. 700, which UNC gave him with a win against Villanova in the 2013 NCAA tournament, and No. 800.

The four years and 100 victories between those milestones had been some of the most difficult of his life: the death of close friends and mentors Smith and Bill Guthridge; the death of his neighbor and best friend Ted Seagroves; the never-ending NCAA investigation and all the baggage that has come with it.

"From 700 to 800, the kids have been my salvation," Williams said. "You guys know the junk that's been going on. I've taken a lot of it personally, and I was not involved.

"But if it wasn't for the kids, and the way they've made me feel — they've made me really enjoy coaching, enjoy life every day. That's a special thing."

Williams didn't mention the stakes before Monday. He didn't tell his players that a victory against Syracuse would place him on an esteemed list of coaches in college basketball history.

He didn't want his players feeling any sort of pressure. They knew anyway, though, said Theo Pinson, the junior forward.

"We all knew about it," he said, "So we tried to do everything we could to take care of business."Joel Berry, the junior point guard, said he was "honored" to be a part of it. He and his teammates crowded around Williams and shared the moment on the court on Monday night. The video tribute played on high above. In the front row Baldwin took in the scene, 52 years after the start of a relationship that changed his life, and Williams', too. ■

Roy Williams and the Tar Heels faithful watch a montage of the head coach's memorable career achievements from the path to 800 victories. (Robert Willett - rwillett@newsobserver.com)

ROY WILLIAMS

With Distinctive Fashion Sense, Williams 'Epitomizes Carolina-ness' from Head to Toe

By Andrew Carter • January 20, 2017

The jacket is five or six years old now, and it's the one piece Roy Williams wears that elicits the strongest reactions. Some people love it, the boldness, and others who say they love it might be lying. Williams has heard both sides, and at first he wasn't even all that sure what to think of it.

"He didn't wear it much in the beginning," said Alexander Julian, who designed the jacket, and many others that Williams often wears. "I'm not sure he even wore it the first year he had it. And then he wore it and he got a lot of compliments. And he won."

Williams, the North Carolina coach, wore it on Monday night during the Tar Heels' 85-68 victory against Syracuse. It was his 800th victory as a Division I coach — a milestone victory — and as he's known to do, he picked out something special for the occasion.

The jacket he wore — "strong jacket," Julian, 68, said — is made from custom English fabric, and is a gingham plaid lambswool. Streaks of Carolina blue intersect, leaving dark gray squares. At Julian's on Franklin Street, which is celebrating its 75th anniversary, a swatch of the fabric sits out on a table near the back.

The fabric, cut into a small square, is next to a picture of Williams wearing the jacket during a game. Nearby is a larger spool of the fabric, and if a customer

is so inclined he can be fitted, the way Williams was, and own the same custom jacket for $2,000.

The fabric is so popular — so much the subject of questions, and curiosity — it stays out in view.

"Enough people ask about that, that I have to keep it handy," said Bart Fox, the store's men's manager. Fox is Julian's nephew and the grandson of Maurice Julian, who opened this store, originally on the other side of Franklin, as a small haberdashery in 1942.

When Williams wore the coat the night of his 800th victory, Julian took notice. He felt proud.

"I loved it," he said.

Then again, he feels such a connection with a lot of what Williams, 66, wears, because he is responsible for perhaps as much as half of Williams' game day wardrobe. Williams' relationship with Julian's, the store, dates to when Williams was a student at UNC. He at least knew of it back then.

His relationship with Julian, the designer, dates to when Williams was an assistant coach under Dean Smith in the late 1970s and '80s. Julian remembers meeting Williams in his days as an assistant, and when Williams coached at Kansas he bought suits from one of Julian's friends in Lawrence.

Williams returned to UNC in 2003 to become the Tar Heels' head coach, and he and Julian, the father of

Roy Williams yells instructions at his team during a narrow 80-78 win against Pittsburgh on Tuesday, January 31, 2017 at the Smith Center. (Robert Willett - rwillett@newsobserver.com)

UNC's argyle design, grew closer. In the years since, Williams has become one of the most stylish college basketball coaches in the country, what with his affinity for plaids and pastels.

Julian isn't behind all of Williams' outfits, but he's behind many of them — if not most of them. These days, he visits with Williams before every season. He brings garment bags filled with suits and jackets, shirts. He brings ties and accessories.

He brings Fox, too, and he handles the measurements and makes sure everything fits to Williams' liking. Williams has his preferences — the pants pleated, for instance, and the jackets with enough room for him to pace the sideline, or stomp around it, as it were, in comfort.

Julian likes to say that "Roy knows what he likes." But Julian knows what Williams likes, too, even before Williams might realize that he agrees. Take the jacket Williams wore the night of his 800th victory, for instance.

"If I believe in it and I want to push him, he'll listen," Julian said. "He knows. He's an expert on himself, and he knows what he likes and what he doesn't like, and he makes a quick decision."

UNC CONNECTION

Williams doesn't wear Julian's clothes exclusively. His game attire, he said during an interview before the season, is about half Julian's, half Peter Millar. And yet Williams and Julian are in some ways, many ways, tied together given they both share the same kind of deep connection with UNC.

The Julian's store, after all, has been a Franklin Street mainstay for more than seven decades. Maurice Julian graduated from UNC in 1938 and made clothes for Choo Choo Justice. Alexander Julian attended UNC and was part of the class of 1967, but dropped out before graduating to begin his career.

When Dean Smith wanted to redesign UNC's uniforms in the early 1990s he turned to Julian, who by then had designed the Charlotte Hornets' first uniform. A prototype of it, the last remaining original, Fox said, is on display on a mannequin in a corner at Julian's. Nearby is a prototype of Julian's original UNC jersey, the first one with the argyle side panels that have become iconic.

At Julian's there are homages to UNC history all around, if you know where to look. Sometimes, Fox said, people come in asking specifically about a jacket they saw Williams wear, or a tie. The ties are arranged in a part of the store that is known as "Roy's closet," because he's worn so many of them.

There are the ties he wore during the 2008 and 2009 national semifinals — and the ones from both his championship victories, in 2005 and 2009. There's another with pink squares popping out of a multi-blue background. At first only one of those ties had ever been made, just for Williams.

Then, Fox said, "Every time he wore it on TV, we'd be flooded with phone calls."

And so they made more. Now for $95, anyone can buy "Roy's Pink Windowpane."

Williams' ties are one thing. Some of his jackets, though, are Roy originals, one of a kind.

That doesn't stop the imitators — or perhaps the inspired — from inquiring about the latest piece they saw Williams wearing. Ask Julian just how much of his stuff Williams owns, and the answer doesn't come easily, if it's even an answerable question at all.

"Through the last 10 years," Julian said, "between the socks and pants and cufflinks, ties, dress shirts, sports shirts, pocket squares, sport coats, suits, sweaters, sweater vests … It's a wonderful representation. I would say he epitomizes Carolina-ness, in his style."

Williams has "no idea" how many jackets he owns. "A lot," he said.

'COUNTRY CLUB JACKETS'

Basketball coaches, both in the pros and in college, are the most fashionable men in sports, at least during competition. They stand in contrast to baseball managers, whose uniforms often look comically out of place on the middle-aged, or older.

Many football coaches, meanwhile, favor the sort of attire that might best be described as Mowing the Lawn Chic. Then there are basketball coaches, with their pressed slacks, cufflinks, shined shoes.

Still, much of what they wear can all sort of look the same, one bench of dark, personality-less suits

With his unique, locally-crafted suits, head coach Roy Williams represents North Carolina and its community. (Robert Willett - rwillett@newsobserver.com)

bleeding into the next, an assembly line of easily-forgettable business wear. Williams is an outlier with a style Julian describes as "cool traditional."

Stilman White, the Tar Heels' senior guard who has been around Williams longer than any of his teammates, put it another way. White smiled while he gave the description after a recent UNC victory.

"He likes the country club jackets," White said.

Sometimes Williams keeps it simple. Coach anywhere from 35 to 40 games per season, and not all the jackets and ties are going to be memorable. And yet Williams' stand out enough, whether it's with that gingham plaid lambswool coat or another brown plaid number that had White searching.

He scrolled down the screen on his phone, looking at the images from a Google search. He found it.

"I remember this one," White said. "This one right here. Remember the brown one?"

"I hate that one," said Nate Britt, the senior guard, looking over White's shoulder.

"I like that one," White said. "Brown. Oh, yeah. Right there."

Players may disagree about the fashion sense of some of Williams' choices. At least once earlier this season, though, junior forward Theo Pinson said there was collective appreciation among the team for an outfit Pinson described as "real smooth."

He couldn't remember the jacket, exactly, only that it was "bluish." Yet Pinson and his teammates know.

They know that when Williams dresses a certain way, the stakes might be higher.

"He's got his own taste, for sure," White said. "And we appreciate that. We know when he's wearing a fly jacket like that, he's ready to coach us up for a big game."

A NEW FABRIC

For the game earlier this month against N.C. State, the school and team Williams might want to beat more than any other, Williams broke out one of Julian's newer jackets. From a distance, it looked like a heavy tweed coat.

As Julian described it, though, the coat is "cotton tweed" — a new fabric that Julian said he recently invented. The tweed pattern is printed on lightweight stretch cotton, a "digital printed Donegal tweed,"

Julian said, speaking his native language: fashion.

"And then," Julian said, "Just for him, nobody else has this, but I put Carolina blue-dyed pearl buttons on the jacket."

The Tar Heels won by 51 points, and so Williams will likely wear the jacket again. And again.

He has relationships like that with some of his clothes. That's part of the reason why he continues to wear the jacket he wore on Monday night — it brings back good memories, ones of winning. Williams can tell you about the suits he had on during UNC's two national title victories.

He can remember ones he wore in less happier times, too. A few years ago, Williams wore a new suit for the first time for a home game against Miami. He thought the suit was "pretty neat," he said, but its debut coincided with a defeat.

"And I've never worn it since," Williams said.

He's not sure if he'll ever wear it again for a game but he thought of another utility for it:

"I can wear it to a funeral."

MANY OPTIONS

Some of Julian's designs are undoubtedly among the collection Williams has banned from his rotation. Julian said he's "afraid to ask" what happens to those cursed clothes, though Williams simply keeps them in his closest with all the rest, a mental Do Not Wear tag attached to them.

It's not as if Williams lacks for options. Julian is working on something new all the time, and he designs clothes with Williams in mind, just for him. Julian is already thinking ahead to next year, the way a coach might think about an incoming prospect.

There's a prized new jacket in the works. Williams hasn't seen the fabric yet, but no matter.

"I guarantee you he'll love it," Julian said.

He's been wrong before, though. Julian always liked that lambswool gingham — the one Williams wore for his 800th victory — but it took Williams some time to come around.

Pinson recently called that jacket "the classic one."

"You know what I'm talking about," he said. "That's a classic. I know it's a big-time game when he's wearing that one." ∎

North Carolina coach Roy Williams watches his team during the Tar Heels' second-round win over Arkansas in the NCAA Tournament. (Robert Willett - rwillett@newsobserver.com)

2
POINT GUARD

JOEL BERRY II

Berry Brings Trademark Intensity to Tar Heels Squad

By Andrew Carter • January 31, 2017

When North Carolina returned home after its defeat at Miami on Saturday, Joel Berry knew where he wanted to go and knew he wanted to be there alone. No teammates. No managers or coaches. The Tar Heels had lost and Berry had played poorly, and on the inside the anger simmered.

"So intense," Justin Jackson, the Tar Heels' junior forward, said of Berry on Tuesday night after UNC's 80-78 victory against Pittsburgh. "... With how intense he is, I think he can sometimes get more down on himself than he probably should. But at times that helps."

It helped on Tuesday, for instance, after a couple of marathon, solo shooting sessions helped Berry regain his touch, and his spirt. The Tar Heels' victory against the Panthers at the Smith Center will be remembered for how close it came — only a two-point win against the ACC's last-place team.

And yet it easily could have been a stunning loss, and perhaps would have been, if not for Berry's turnaround — from two points on 0-for-8 shooting at Miami to 19 points and five 3-pointers against Pitt, which was in it until its final shot, a 3-point attempt from Jamel Artis, went awry at the buzzer.

Afterward UNC coach Roy Williams bemoaned his team's defense, which allowed Pitt to shoot 55.6 percent.

Williams surmised that some of the media members covering his team, not the most athletic bunch, might have been as comfortable at the Smith Center free throw line as UNC's post players were guarding the Panthers' smaller players on the perimeter.

"Somehow, some way," Williams said, "I've got to figure out a way to do a better job coaching on the defensive end of the floor."

If defense nearly cost the Tar Heels (20-4, 8-2 ACC) a victory then Jackson, who finished with 20 points, and Berry preserved it. Berry's resurgence was especially encouraging, given what happened just days earlier in South Florida.

His performance at Miami was his worst of the season, and in the middle of it he collected a technical foul amid an uncharacteristic verbal outburst. Berry acknowledged he allowed emotion to overcome his judgment when he said something an official didn't appreciate.

Back in Chapel Hill on Saturday night, Berry channeled his frustration. He walked into the Smith Center, empty and quiet, and connected his phone to the sound system. He rolled in an apparatus he described as "the gun," which fed him passes and tracked his shooting percentage.

And he remained in the gym, alone, until he

Joel Berry II (2) drives against Florida State's Xavier Rathan-Mayes (22) and Michael Ojo. North Carolina went on to win the home game 96-83. (Robert Willett - rwillett@newsobserver.com)

attempted 500 shots. All the while the musical playlist on his phone sounded through the Smith Center speakers, Berry in his own world. He said he attempted to correct his mental energy, and he envisioned his shots going in — unlike the scene, eight times over, at Miami.

"Sometimes you can have all these good games and you get on a little high," said Berry, who has played well enough this season to become a contender for ACC Player of the Year honors. "So that was one of my lows and it kind of made me refocus. It's not a bad thing but at the time it was because of how I played.

"But it's just life. Sometimes you have lows and it kind of gets you back on track."

That was Berry attempting to find the right track, hoisting those 500 shots. He came back the next day, on Sunday, and did it again. Except once he reached 500 shot attempts, Berry said he attempted 100 more.

The setting was the same: the otherwise empty Smith Center, the shooting machine, his music playing through the speakers. Berry during his three seasons at UNC has in some ways become the Tar Heels' emotional pulse. He doesn't provide the electrical current that Theo Pinson does, yet Berry's intensity is likely unmatched.

Berry didn't have it on Saturday. Then again, Williams didn't recognize much of anything about Berry.

"The guy who showed up on Saturday was not Joel Berry," Williams said. "And I thought we had some alien that climbed up in his body. But I think it was Joel at pregame, at shoot-around today."

Berry needed all of 13 seconds on Tuesday to score more points against Pittsburgh (12-10, 1-8) than he scored all of Saturday at Miami. His first 3-point attempt against the Panthers went in, and all five of his 3s came in the first 24 minutes.

As unexpected as it was, the Tar Heels needed all of those points. They needed Berry's three-point play, especially, with 98 seconds remaining. Those points came the old-fashioned way — on a layup and a free throw — and the layup brought an end to an ugly stretch in which UNC

Joel Berry II soars to the basket on a fast break during the first half against Wake Forest on January 11, 2017 at Lawrence Joel Coliseum in Winston-Salem.
(Robert Willett - rwillett@newsobserver.com)

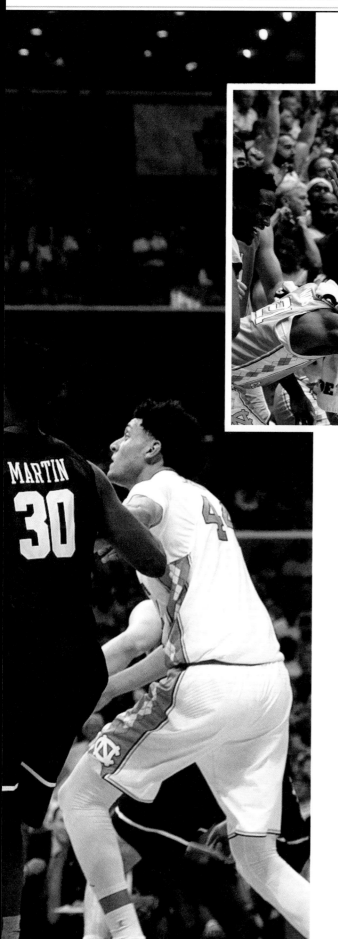

missed nine consecutive shots from the field.

The Tar Heels led by four then but four times during the final 90 seconds Pitt cut UNC's lead to either one point or two. It wasn't over until the Panthers missed their final shot, and yet in some ways UNC's victory began with Berry's first shots, and the hundreds that followed, on Saturday and Sunday.

Williams said Berry "gets so mad at himself" when he plays like he did at Miami. Jackson described the intensity. Isaiah Hicks, the senior forward, described the fight: "Coach always says that's the thing he loves about Joel the most — he's a fighter."

The Tar Heels needed some fight on Tuesday, and needed it perhaps more than anybody could have anticipated. After a couple of long, lonely sessions in this same building, Berry came prepared to provide it. ▪

Opposite: Joel Berry II scores two of his game-high 26 points in the second half of UNC's Sweet Sixteen match-up against Butler. Above: Berry's Tar Heel teammates are ecstatic after a 3-pointer against Duke. (Robert Willett - rwillett@newsobserver.com)

4
FORWARD

ISAIAH HICKS

From 'Deer in the Headlights' to Senior Starter

By Andrew Carter • February 7, 2017

Yes, Roy Williams said on Tuesday, he did remember the play. Two years later he could still see it: the clock winding down at Duke's Cameron Indoor Stadium, North Carolina with a chance to tie the score in overtime, the ball in Isaiah Hicks' hands in the lane, open.

Williams might not have remembered what he said after that 92-90 loss at Duke in 2015. So here's a reminder of how he reacted to that moment — Hicks holding the ball, the seconds ticking away:

"He just didn't realize how open he was. He could have taken one bounce and dunked the ball, probably."

Instead Hicks passed to J.P. Tokoto, who missed a shot on the baseline. Game over.

It was only one play, and Williams on Tuesday warned not to read too much into it. And yet few plays over Hicks' four years are better illustrative of his journey from those too-timid days years ago to where he is now, among the centerpieces of the Tar Heels' offense.

Hicks, the Tar Heels' 6-10 senior forward, reflected on Tuesday. He'll be back in Cameron Indoor Stadium on Thursday night for another UNC-Duke game, his fourth and final one in Durham, and he remembered it, too — freezing in the lane in overtime during his sophomore year.

Hicks seemed bashful about it. He sounded almost embarrassed.

"(Comparing) now to then, I would have shot that shot — no hesitation," he said. "Then it was just being in a (difficult) environment, stuff like that, and I was still in the phase of being the deer in the headlights."

That phase, it turned out, lasted awhile. Hicks arrived at UNC in 2013 amid considerable hype. He'd been an all-state player at Webb High in Oxford, the No. 1 high school prospect in North Carolina. Others with similar accolades might have arrived in college with an inflated sense of confidence.

Hicks had the opposite problem, though. For four years, his teammates and coaches have had to remind him of how good he can be. It was something else during his freshman and sophomore years when, homesick, he often traveled back home on weekends. College seemed to overwhelm him.

Take, for instance, the first time Hicks started a game at UNC. It came in the Bahamas, in the Battle 4 Atlantis, early into his sophomore season.

"I started him three times the first three years, and he about had a heart attack every game I started him," Williams said. "So we had to wait until he got through that. In the Bahamas, he runs over there, and I thought he was dying. I'm looking for a surgeon to get him to calm down."

Hicks shook his head at the memory, smiling a little. He spoke of "getting too excited."

Isaiah Hicks battles for his shot during a UNC win over Syracuse. (Robert Willett - rwillett@newsobserver.com)

And then there was the anxiety and everything that came with the nerves. Like fouls, for instance.

"It was just me psyching myself out," Hicks said.

It has taken Hicks a long time to reach a point of comfort, and confidence.

How long, exactly? He didn't need long to answer on Tuesday.

"It seemed like it took three or four years," he said. "So I would say that's a very long process."

Look at him now. During UNC's past nine games, Hicks is averaging 14.2 points and 6.2 rebounds. Both of those totals are above his season averages. Entering Cameron Indoor Stadium on Thursday night, Hicks is expected to be an important part of the Tar Heels' plans.

If, that is, he remains free of foul trouble. He has recently, anyway. During Hicks' past seven games, he's collected more than three fouls only once — and he finished UNC's victory against Syracuse on Jan. 16 without committing any fouls at all.

That had only happened once earlier this season, and once last season. Some of his teammates seemed incredulous that Hicks, so prone to "silly fouls," as Williams likes to say, had played 30 minutes without a single foul.

"That's crazy, man," Kennedy Meeks, the Tar Heels other starting senior forward, told Hicks after the Syracuse game.

"Zero," Hicks said, repeating his foul total. "Zero!"

"That's wild," Meeks said. "That's crazy. I can't believe that."

As improbable as it was to finish a game without a foul, playing at least 30 minutes in consecutive games might have been even more of an accomplishment for Hicks. And yet he did that, too, during UNC's victories against Pittsburgh and Notre Dame.

It was the first time in his four seasons that Hicks had played that many minutes in consecutive games. And it will be critical, again, on Thursday that he remain on the court at Duke, where Hicks could create a mismatch in UNC's favor if the Blue Devils decide to use a smaller lineup.

"If he's just aggressive when he gets the ball, it's just hard for the defense to guard him," said Justin Jackson, the

North Carolina's Isaiah Hicks (4) faces off against Miami's Ebuka Izundu during the ACC Tournament. Hicks led his team with 19 points in their 78-53 victory.
(Robert Willett - rwillett@newsobserver.com)

Tar Heels' junior forward. "I mean, he's so quick and strong inside, and his athletic ability — for him to be able to finish above the rim — it's big."

Hicks still hears it from his teammates and coaches, he said. They still remind him of how good he can be. Only difference now is Hicks has reached a point where he seems to believe it.

Come Thursday he could well find himself in the same kind of position he was two years ago: time running short, the Tar Heels in need of points, the ball in his hands. Don't expect Hicks to pass this time. ■

Opposite: Isaiah Hicks (4) breaks to the basket ahead of Duke's Luke Kennard (5) for a dunk. Above: Hicks, with teammates Kennedy Meeks and Nate Britt, accepts the South Regional championship trophy following North Carolina's 75-73 victory over Kentucky. (Robert Willett - rwillett@newsobserver.com)

REGULAR SEASON

FEBRUARY 18, 2017 · CHAPEL HILL, NORTH CAROLINA
NORTH CAROLINA 65, VIRGINIA 41

FLYING HIGH

Tar Heels Glad to Have Isaiah Hicks Back After Injury Scare
By Jonathan M. Alexander

If there were any doubts about North Carolina senior Isaiah Hicks' health coming into the game against Virginia, they were quickly erased.

The 6-9, 242-pound forward, rose for a dunk so high — with 18:14 left in the first half — that it looked like he was looking down at the rim when he reached his peak in the air.

He slammed in two of his 10 points as the crowd rose to its feet in the No. 10 Tar Heels' (23-5, 11-3 ACC) 65-41 win over the Cavaliers (18-8, 8-6).

"Glad to see Isaiah is starting to look more like himself again," UNC coach Roy Williams said. "He's feeling better right now."

This was Hicks' second game back since injuring his hamstring on Feb. 8 while he was running a fast-break drill in practice. He ended up sitting out in the Tar Heels' 86-78 loss to Duke the next night.

"It wasn't good," Hicks said of having to sit out. "I feel like I could have helped the team out a little bit."

Since that loss, the Tar Heels, first in the ACC, have won two straight, both by 24 points.

Hicks said he no longer feels hampered by the injury.

"It feels better," he said. "Completely better, honestly. Out there running and stuff, I don't feel it."

Hicks finished the game with 10 points and eight rebounds

"Just having him out there is more effective than having him on the bench," junior guard Joel Berry said. "He plays hard. He gets to the backboards, and he just does his job.

"So with him out there, it just gives us another option."

Hicks averages 12.6 points and 5.4 rebounds per game and shoots 61 percent from the floor. The down-low pressure from Hicks and senior forward Kennedy Meeks helped open the floor for the guards.

Virginia double-teamed the post whenever Hicks and Meeks (6-10, 260) got the ball. Because of that, the two big men were able to kick the ball out and find the open man. Senior forward Justin Jackson was the beneficiary of many of those double teams.

Jackson scored 18 points in the first half and finished with 20 points total.

Junior wing Theo Pinson said having Hicks takes the pressure off other players on defense. He said Hicks can guard players smaller than him, which makes it so Jackson and Pinson don't have to fight over screens. With Hicks, the two can just switch.

Meeks agreed.

"I think that definitely could have helped us a lot at Duke, but God already made his will, and he didn't want him to play," Meeks said with a smile. "It's unfortunate that he wasn't there. I'm pretty sure it would have been a different outcome if he was." ▪

Forward Isaiah Hicks puts up a shot over the Virginia defense. Hicks scored 10 points in the Tar Heels' 65-41 victory. (Robert Willett - rwillett@newsobserver.com)

After a recent hamstring setback, senior Isaiah Hicks looked back in form with a dunk against Virginia. (Robert Willett - rwillett@newsobserver.com)

REGULAR SEASON
FEBRUARY 22, 2017 • CHAPEL HILL, NORTH CAROLINA
NORTH CAROLINA 74, LOUISVILLE 63

SEIZING THE DAY

UNC Takes Control of ACC Race with Win Over Louisville

By Andrew Carter

This wasn't exactly the way North Carolina coach Roy Williams drew it up — his team missing a bunch of shots early, the Tar Heels slow to score on the interior, Isaiah Hicks in foul trouble, Theo Pinson shooting (and making) 3-pointers … but Williams said recently the Tar Heels had to find comfort winning in a variety of ways, and so this, too, was something new.

The Tar Heels in the second half at the Smith Center pulled away for a 74-63 victory against Louisville, and UNC did it with Hicks in foul trouble and with Kennedy Meeks, its other starting big man, fumbling away passes. The Tar Heels did it with Pinson, not known for his perimeter shooting, making his second 3-pointer of the night.

And they did it with Justin Jackson, the junior forward, playing a prominent role, as usual. Jackson, one of four Tar Heels who scored in double figures, led UNC with 21 points, and at least his contributions went according to plan. Jackson's 3-pointer with a little less than five minutes remaining gave the Tar Heels a 64-49 lead, and it prompted Louisville coach Rick Pitino to call a timeout.

By then, though, the No. 8 Tar Heels (24-5, 12-3 ACC), who began the game mired in a miserable shooting funk, appeared firmly in control. The Cardinals in the final few minutes never trailed by fewer than eight points, and UNC celebrated its second consecutive victory in which its defense was as integral a component to its success as its offense.

UNC during its 65-41 victory against Virginia held the Cavaliers to 27.8 percent shooting from the field. The numbers weren't that impressive against Louisville (22-6, 10-5), but the Cardinals, whose struggles on the road continued, went through shooting woes of their own and shot 43.3 percent overall.

One of the loudest moments in the Smith Center came early in the game, when the score of Syracuse's victory against Duke appeared on the video boards high in the corners of the arena. UNC fans looked up, saw the news of the Orange's 78-75 victory, and collectively released a loud, long roar.

Syracuse's victory had practical implications for UNC, too, aside from the pleasure it brought its supporters. The Orange's win meant that the Tar Heels, with a victory of their own, could take a full two-game lead atop the ACC standings.

And so now, with three games left to play, the Tar Heels lead Louisville, Duke, Florida State and Notre Dame by two games in the conference standings.

North Carolina's Tony Bradley splits the Louisville defense during the second half of the February 22 win at the Smith Center. (Robert Willett - rwillett@newsobserver.com)

Those four teams all are tied for second place, with a 10-5 conference record, and only three of them will receive double-byes in the upcoming ACC tournament.

UNC led 33-30 at halftime, despite missing 15 of its first 18 shots from the field. The Tar Heels led by seven, twice, early in the second half — the last of those times with 17½ minutes remaining. At the time the Tar Heels had momentum and the crowd was into it, and it appeared, briefly, as though UNC might seize the kind of control that's difficult to wrestle away.

But then all of that was gone in an instant — or in about 90 seconds. That's how long Louisville needed to erase that seven-point difference and tie the game, which it did on Donovan Mitchell's 3-pointer with about 16 minutes remaining.

Gradually UNC extended its lead again, and it led 51-43 with 11½ minutes remaining after Pinson's second 3-pointer. It was the first time since Dec. 30, 2015, that Pinson, who finished with 11 points, had made multiple 3-pointers in a game.

With the Tar Heels failing to assert themselves on the interior the way they prefer — they finished with only 26 points in the paint — their perimeter shooting turned out to be instrumental in the victory. UNC, which led by as many 17 points with less than four minutes remaining, made seven 3s, with Jackson accounting for four of those.

In the final seconds the Tar Heels simply dribbled out the clock. They received a standing ovation while they did, and walked off the Smith Center court firmly in control of the race for the ACC's regular season championship. ◼

Louisville's Deng Adel (22) secures an offensive rebound over North Carolina's Theo Pinson (1). Pinson and his teammates' 3-point shooting would prove crucial in the 74-63 victory. (Robert Willett - rwillett@newsobserver.com)

44
FORWARD

JUSTIN JACKSON
UNC's Jackson Unfazed by Hype
By Andrew Carter • February 23, 2017

After another memorable performance in what's becoming a long line of them, Justin Jackson, the North Carolina junior forward, said he tries to enter each game with zen-like mental clarity, and a focus on the things in his life most important to him.

That, he said, would be things like school and family and "not getting caught up in the hype."

"That guys like y'all might write," Jackson said with a smile.

Ignoring the hype, though, is about to become more difficult for Jackson, for it is building. Jackson has been one of the ACC's best, most consistent players this season — but he has thrived in the kind of relative anonymity that belies his role on one of the nation's best teams.

And yet the word, finally, is starting to get out: Jackson might be as good as anyone in the country. Jackson during the Tar Heels' 74-63 victory against Louisville on Wednesday night finished with 21 points — the ninth time in an ACC game this season that he's scored at least 20.

He made four 3-pointers, the 10th time this season that he's made at least that many. And he played so well that Rick Pitino, the Louisville coach, offered effusive praise afterward.

"The two players I'm most impressed with in college basketball this year — one, never gets any credit," Pitino said. "Justin Jackson to me should be one of the key guys for the Wooden Award."

UNC supporters might not want to hear the other name Pitino mentioned: Duke's Luke Kennard. Unlike Jackson, though, Kennard for weeks has been a part of the national conversation for player of the year awards and All-American honors.

For a while now Kennard has received recognition. Now Jackson is earning his.

"I don't know which guy I would pick for player of the year," Pitino said. "They're both awesome."

After Wednesday, Jackson is averaging 18.7 points per game, which ranks seventh in the conference. He has made an average of 2.7 3-pointers per game, which ranks second in the ACC behind Syracuse's Andrew White.

Jackson is making 39.6 percent of his 3-point attempts — an improvement of about 10 percent from last season. Since his freshman year, when Jackson made 30.4 percent of his 3-point attempts, he has become one of the most improved -- if not the most improved -- shooters in school history.

Jackson made 63 3-pointers during his first two years at UNC. He has made 78 this season, and with

During the 2016-17 season, UNC's Justin Jackson showed he was one to watch not only in the ACC, but across all of college hoops. Jackson was named the 2017 ACC Player of the Year and first-team All-ACC. (Ethan Hyman - ehyman@newsobserver.com)

18 more 3-pointers Jackson would set the school record for most in a season. Meanwhile, Jackson is earning more attention just about every time he plays.

For a while this year he thrived in obscurity, relative to his accomplishments. No longer, though. After the victory against Louisville on Wednesday, someone told Jackson what Pitino had said — that he should be a leading candidate for national player of the year honors.

As he often tries to do, Jackson dismissed the hype.

"Those type of awards, I'll let y'all talk about them. Obviously, there's guys like Luke, Donovan's playing great," he said of Louisville's Donovan Mitchell. "There's a bunch of guys in the ACC that are extremely good. So for me, I'll let y'all talk about who's the front runner, who's in the conversation. I'm not really worried about all of that.

"I'm worried about the fact that we're two games in first and we can still control our own destiny." ▪

Opposite: Justin Jackson (44) drives to the basket against Pittsburgh's Sheldon Jeter (21). (Robert Willett - rwillett@newsobserver.com) Above: Jackson reacts after sinking yet another 3-point shot. The junior would go on to set the UNC record for most 3-pointers in a season in 2017. (Chuck Liddy - cliddy@newsobserver.com)

Justin Jackson's stand-out play earned
him first-team All-American honors.
(Robert Willett - rwillett@newsobserver.com)

REGULAR SEASON

MARCH 4, 2017 · CHAPEL HILL, NORTH CAROLINA
NORTH CAROLINA 90, DUKE 83

'CAPABLE OF AMAZING'
Tar Heels Outlast Blue Devils in Memorable ACC Finale
By Luke DeCock

The ceiling is the roof, Michael Jordan informed the Smith Center crowd at halftime. It may be easier for semioticians to figure out what exactly MJ's malaprop meant than it will be for anyone else to separate North Carolina and Duke, two teams a total of one point apart after splitting their two regular-season meetings.

Fortunately, they're on conflicting flight paths toward Friday night's first ACC semifinal, if both advance in Brooklyn. This feels like the kind of season that needs a third meeting, after two games decided by missed free throws and extraordinary individual performances. It might just get it.

This game had everything: 23 lead changes, a Grayson Allen technical foul for elbowing Brandon Robinson, Roy Williams shushing his own student section for an "overrated" chant directed at Duke freshman Harry Giles and Joel Berry's second annual recognition that the calendar has changed from February to March. Just as Jayson Tatum took over the second half in Duke's win in Durham, Berry was the difference Saturday night, with 19 of his 28 in the first half to outduel Luke Kennard's 28 in a 90-83 win.

A year after Berry emerged as North Carolina's best player in the postseason, it felt like he was getting a headstart on it this time around.

"Just a little bit," Berry said.

It wasn't just Berry and Kennard. Justin Jackson, after starting 0-for-6 from 3-point range, converted his seventh try to give North Carolina the lead for good, then passed out of a double team to Isaiah Hicks for an easy basket on the next possession. Hicks, who missed the first meeting with a hamstring injury, had 21 points in the rematch and was one of eight different players in double figures, even if Berry stole the show.

"(Berry) is capable of amazing," Duke coach Mike Krzyzewski said. "There were a few players on the court who are capable of amazing."

There was a lot of that in both games this season. Last season, too. Duke pulled the upset in Chapel Hill a year ago even after Matt Jones' ankle injury left the Blue Devils down to six players; North Carolina's seniors won in Cameron for the first time in the return game, clinching the regular-season title in the process.

The first meeting this season turned on Berry missing the front end of a one-and-one, followed by a Tatum 3-pointer at the other end and another Berry miss. This one turned on Allen missing a pair of free throws that would have made it a two-point game with two minutes to go, Berry hitting a pull-up jumper in Allen's face before the misses and banging one off the glass immediately after.

Amid all the excellence, those misses made the difference. When so much is happening at such a high level, it's the flaws that catch the light.

"You saw a game where a lot of guys played well.

Joel Berry II scored 28 against Duke in a show-stopping performance. (Robert Willett - rwillett@newsobserver.com)

That's it," Krzyzewski said. "Sometimes it's not nuclear science here. It's that easy."

North Carolina made it look easy this season, even if the Tar Heels avoided some of the ACC's best teams on the road. They were still two games better than anyone else and had the outright regular-season title secured for the second straight year even before tipoff Saturday, which is how Kennedy Meeks ended up with a net around his neck after the game.

"A lot of guys have been here before, and we wanted to do this again, and we did," North Carolina's Theo Pinson said. "Now, we have to go take care of business in the ACC tournament."

Duke still needed a win not only to extend its streak in Chapel Hill to three games but avoid a Wednesday appearance in Brooklyn. The Blue Devils are instead the fifth seed, facing the N.C. State-Clemson winner, with Louisville awaiting in the quarterfinals. And then, if the cosmic tumblers click into place, North Carolina would await Friday night after facing the Syracuse-Miami winner Thursday.

It just feels like these teams deserve another meeting. They've earned it. We all have. It's not nuclear science, not when the ceiling is the roof. ■

Above: Senior Kennedy Meeks wipes back tears as he addresses the home crowd following the Tar Heels' win. (Robert Willett - rwillett@newsobserver.com) Opposite: UNC forward Justin Jackson has his fist-half shot blocked during the tense 90-83 win. (Chuck Liddy - cliddy@newsobserver.com)

UNC forward Tony Bradley (5) blocks Duke
forward Amile Jefferson (21) as the Tar Heels
battled hard to defeat the Blue Devils 90-83.
(Chuck Liddy - cliddy@newsobserver.com)

ACC TOURNAMENT QUARTERFINALS
MARCH 9, 2017 · NEW YORK, NEW YORK
NORTH CAROLINA 78, MIAMI 53

ROUNDING INTO FORM

UNC Takes it Up a Level in Victory Against Miami

By Andrew Carter

It was about a year ago at this time, during the ACC tournament, when North Carolina began to transform into the team it became during its March run to the national championship game. The Tar Heels then played with more precision, more urgency, more aggressiveness.

They played then a lot like they did here during their 78-53 victory against Miami in the ACC tournament quarterfinals at the Barclays Center. With the victory, the Tar Heels advanced to the tournament semifinals, where they'll play against either Louisville or Duke.

What transpired was the short-term benefit for UNC. The long-term benefits, though, could be more wide-ranging. A year ago, UNC used victories like this one as a catalyst all March.

The Tar Heels' performance offered a significant contrast to their 77-62 loss at Miami on Jan. 28. In that defeat, UNC shot 35 percent and finished with its second-fewest points of the season. UNC on Thursday equaled that scoring total with about nine minutes to play.

The Tar Heels (27-6), the top seed in the ACC tournament, scored their 62nd point in incredulous fashion, on a 3-pointer from Theo Pinson. At least, that's how it will show up in the official play-by-play. In reality, Pinson was attempting to throw a lob pass into the interior.

Instead the pass fell through the rim. Pinson stood for a moment and stared with a blank expression. He didn't seem to believe that his pass went in. At the time, it gave UNC a 62-46 lead — its largest of the game.

About four minutes later, with the Tar Heels in the midst of a 14-1 run over the span of about 5½ minutes, the Tar Heels led 71-47. By then UNC, which has played in the past two ACC tournament championship games, was well on its way to the semifinals.

The positives for UNC, aside from the final outcome, included Isaiah Hicks' overall performance, the execution on offense, and its defensive urgency. Hicks led UNC with 19 points, one of four Tar Heels players in double figures.

Overall, UNC shot 53.1 percent — nearly 20 percentage points better than in the defeat at Miami during the regular season. And, defensively, the Tar Heels attacked passing lanes and hounded the Hurricanes (20-11) both on the perimeter and the interior.

In the final minutes, UNC coach Roy Williams called on some of his reserves who play only sparingly. One who entered the game was Stilman White, the senior guard. He made a 3-pointer not longer after he stepped on the court, and the Tar Heels' onslaught continued. ∎

Isaiah Hicks (4) dunks over Miami's Davon Reed (5) on a fast break. Hicks led North Carolina with 19 points in their 78-53 victory at the Barclays Center in Brooklyn, New York. (Robert Willett - rwillett@newsobserver.com)

North Carolina's Theo Pinson (1) gets a dunk during the first half of his team's ACC tournament quarterfinal match-up with Miami. (Robert Willett - rwillett@newsobserver.com)

MARCH 10, 2017 · NEW YORK, NEW YORK
DUKE 93, NORTH CAROLINA 83

SECOND-HALF COLLAPSE

Duke's Second-Half Charge Leads Blue Devils Past UNC, Into ACC Tournament Title Game

By Andrew Carter

Duke has been an enigma for long stretches this season, a team whose considerable talent has been tested by injuries and inconsistency and, at times, by Grayson Allen's controversial antics. After all of it, though, the Blue Devils are one victory away from an ACC championship after their 93-83 victory against North Carolina in the ACC tournament semifinals.

The Blue Devils (26-8), the tournament's No. 5 seed, trailed by 13 points late in the first half, and by 13, again, with a little less than 14 minutes remaining. At the time the Tar Heels led 61-48 after Kennedy Meeks, the senior forward, made a layup, which gave him 19 points. UNC (27-7), then the tournament's top seed, seemed as though it might be on its way, thanks in large part to Meeks and its ability to score inside.

But even then, the Tar Heels found themselves in perilous position, what with Joel Berry, the junior point guard, on the bench with four fouls. Duke increased its defensive intensity, the Tar Heels withered offensively, and after that Meeks layup Duke outscored UNC 29-11 during the next 11½ minutes and led 77-72 with 3½ minutes remaining.

From there, the Blue Devils' lead only became wider. It grew as large as 11 during the final two minutes, with many in a sold-out crowd at the Barclays Center, which is hosting the tournament for the first time, standing and chanting, "Let's go Duke." When the Blue Devils were at their best, it often sounded like a Duke home game.

With the victory, Duke advanced to the ACC tournament championship game for the first time since 2014, when it lost against Virginia. The Blue Devils haven't won the tournament since 2011, when they defeated UNC in the championship game.

Before Friday, that was also the most recent time these teams played in the ACC tournament. Duke, led on Friday by Jayson Tatum's 24 points and Luke Kennard's 20, has now defeated the Tar Heels in their past six tournament meetings. UNC hasn't beaten Duke in the ACC tournament since 1998.

It appeared like that stretch of tournament futility against Duke would end for UNC. The Tar Heels controlled most of the first half, and exerted their will on the inside, where they outscored Duke 32-10 in the paint during the first 20 minutes. Those 32 points on

Isaiah Hicks' 19-point performance was not enough to lift UNC over Duke in the ACC tournament semifinals. (Robert Willett - rwillett@newsobserver.com)

the interior were only two fewer than UNC scored in the entirety of its defeat at Duke on Feb. 9.

Meeks, though, didn't score after that layup with about 14 minutes to play. And with Berry sitting out for about 10 minutes after committing his fourth foul, the Tar Heels' offense lacked its usual rhythm while the Blue Devils increased their defensive pressure.

UNC, led by Meeks and Isaiah Hicks, both of whom finished with 19 points, shot only 28.6 percent during the second half, after shooting 55.6 percent in the first half. The game completely reversed course after halftime, and Duke's victory denied UNC its third consecutive appearance in the ACC championship game. ■

Above: North Carolina's Joel Berry II reacts after missing a shot late in the second half against Duke. (Robert Willett - rwillett@newsobserver.com) Opposite: Duke guard Frank Jackson (15) gets his shot blocked by UNC forward Kennedy Meeks (3). (Chuck Liddy - cliddy@newsobserver.com)

UNFINISHED BUSINESS

Tar Heels Seek Redemption for Last Year's Title Loss

By Andrew Carter · March 16, 2017

This is what the end looked like: Kennedy Meeks in front of his locker, tears streaming down his cheeks, while Brice Johnson stared at the floor, while Marcus Paige answered question after question about the heartbreak, surrounded by microphones, while Roy Williams and the North Carolina coaching staff sat outside in a small hallway, frozen, stunned, unblinking.

That's how it looked in the aftermath of the Tar Heels' 77-74 loss on a last-second shot to Villanova early last April in the national championship game. Now nearly a year has gone by, and the time has arrived that UNC has so desperately wanted to experience again — the NCAA tournament. The beginning of what the Tar Heels hope is a new, long run.

However long it lasts, it will begin here on Friday. UNC (27-7), the No. 1 seed in the South Region, will play against 16th-seeded Texas Southern (23-11). By the time tip-off arrives around 4 p.m., 347 days will have passed since the tears and the frozen stares, since the agony that followed one of the most wrenching defeats in college basketball history.

In the days between then and now, how often did the Tar Heels think about it? How often did those who returned relive that defeat, only to imagine the second chance — the last chance, for some playing in their final NCAA tournament — that has now arrived?

"It pops up a lot," Meeks, the senior forward, said in the Tar Heels' locker room on Thursday. "Just because you don't want to get to that point, and then it happens again."

In the aftermath a year ago, Meeks was inconsolable. He spoke through his tears and his sobs about his disappointment — about letting down then-seniors Paige, Johnson and Joel James.

Now Meeks is the senior. And this is his final NCAA tournament.

"I know I don't want me or the other seniors, or anyone on this team to feel the way that I did," he said.

Meeks is perhaps the most active member of the team's group text message thread. Every member of the team is on it and Meeks, according to junior point guard Joel Berry, sends out messages "twice or triple times" the rate of anyone else.

Sometimes Meeks asks his teammates if they want to get something to eat. Or if "anybody is trying to do this, that," Berry said. The messages got to be so much, Berry said, that sometimes he sets his phone on "do not disturb" mode.

Every time those messages — or any others — pop up, the Tar Heels receive a reminder. The title of their

Head coach Roy Williams tosses an autographed basketball back to a fan in the stands ahead of North Carolina's match-up with Butler in the NCAA South Region semifinals. (Robert Willett - rwillett@newsobserver.com)

group text is "redemption," which is the name Justin Jackson gave it back in the summer, a few months after the loss in the national championship.

Different players defined the idea of redemption in their own ways on Thursday. For Jackson the word has come to mean "getting a national championship back, where we almost were."

"Not many things do you get to have redos," said Jackson, the junior wing forward who earned ACC Player of the Year honors. "And Brice and Marcus, they didn't get to have a redo. Joel (James) didn't get to have a redo. But for us, we're blessed enough to be back in this position where we are.

"And we've worked our butts off all year."

"Year" didn't mean the past five months, since the start of practice. It meant the past 11 months, since the end of last season.

After that defeat, nobody said much afterward. What could be said?

Williams addressed his players, like he does after every game. He told them, he said months later, to "use this as fuel" throughout the off-season, to keep the burning embers of despair aflame long after the immediate pain subsided. And yet Williams didn't necessarily need to say that, either.

Everyone knew.

Even those who played their final college game that night knew that, in some ways, the ending to last season represented the immediate beginning of this one. They wouldn't be around to experience it but they understood, anyway: The quest to return began as soon as last season ended.

"I think the crazy thing about how our season ended last year, is that, like, what's understood doesn't have to be explained," Paige said during a recent phone interview. "It's almost like we didn't have to say anything, because they felt that going into this year, that they had to get back."

The desire to return has been the one unifying force driving the Tar Heels all season. It drove them even before the season began.

The goal provided Jackson inspiration during his grueling, sweaty summer workouts — sometimes all-day affairs at the Smith Center. The desire to return to the championship game, and to win it this time, helped forward Isaiah Hicks decide to return to school for his senior season. It helped Theo Pinson, the junior forward who suffered a broken foot in the preseason, through his rehab.

Nearly a year ago, the Tar Heels found themselves 4.7 seconds away from entering overtime against Villanova. Paige had just made one of the great shots in NCAA tournament history — a leaning, double-clutching 3-pointer from beyond the top of the key. It tied the game. It sent seat cushions flying. It sent people wearing light blue into delirium, whether they were in NRG Stadium or in their living room.

And then it was over. Villanova's Kris Jenkins did Paige one better, and at the buzzer.

Now there is a sense of unfinished business. Of not just wanting to win, but needing to win.

"To not only do it for us, the guys that can't play anymore," Paige said, "but also to avenge what we thought was a championship year, a championship team."

Paige, who is remembered, among other things, for the sentimental, emotional senior day speech he gave early last March, didn't leave his teammates with any sort of parting words after the national championship game. There was no rah-rah speech, nothing that could be slapped on a T-shirt or woven into a team slogan.

Some things don't need to be articulated, though. Wasn't it obvious, after all?

"We didn't really have to say much," he said. "It was kind of like, they knew that — they used that as motivation right away from the beginning of the year."

In the preseason, it was all some of UNC's returnees talked about — making it back to the final

North Carolina's players have been working hard toward another title run since 2016's last-second loss to Villanova in the NCAA tournament finals. (Robert Willett - rwillett@newsobserver.com)

Monday night of the season. At the time, it seemed like some faraway destination.

First, there was an entire season to play, a four-month grind. The Tar Heels weren't always as sharp as they hoped. They stumbled at Georgia Tech and Miami, faded in the final minutes at Duke, lost ugly at Virginia. That was it, though: the entirety of UNC's defeats in conference play.

Even another loss against Duke in the ACC tournament semifinals didn't seem all that bad, given it hastened the arrival of the one tournament the Tar Heels have been preparing for all season long. Now at last the time has come.

"That was the biggest thing for me," Berry, the junior point guard, said, "is being able to get back to this tournament, and be able to make that run again."

He spoke of the journey a year ago. Not just the victories along the way, but "the overall experience," as Berry described it — the time together in the locker room, and the travel and the bonding, three weeks of it before that abrupt, crushing ending.

UNC arrived in Greenville on Wednesday, and on Thursday went through the familiar routine — the pregame media circus and a shootaround in front of the fans, then some time together back at the hotel.

"We wanted to get back into the NCAA tournament as soon as we walked off the court last year," Berry said. "And now that it's here … we know what it takes to get back to that point, and this time we're not going to let it get it taken away from us."

That's UNC's hope, at least. Berry and his teammates on Thursday all embraced the optimism.

This is what a new beginning looked like: The Tar Heels in their locker room, waiting to go onto the court for their open practice, waiting for the moment that now was closer than ever — the start of a journey they hope leads them back. ▪

Joel Berry II (2), Justin Jackson (44) and Isaiah Hicks (4) walk off the court after the devastating 77-74 loss to Villanova (Robert Willett - rwillett@newsobserver.com)

NCAA TOURNAMENT FIRST ROUND

MARCH 17, 2017 · GREENVILLE, SOUTH CAROLINA
NORTH CAROLINA 103, TEXAS SOUTHERN 64

TAKING CARE OF BUSINESS
Top-Seeded UNC Coasts Into Second Round with Win Over Texas Southern

By Andrew Carter

Texas Southern had the Ocean of Soul, its loud and spirited band, which filled this place with enough rhythm to make spectators shimmy in their seats, and the Tigers had oversized heart, too, a lot of it personified by their undersized 5-foot-7, 150-pound freshman point guard.

North Carolina, well — North Carolina had everything else. The Tar Heels' opening game of the NCAA tournament, a mismatched affair between one of the richest schools in college athletics and one that lacks the resources power-conference schools take for granted, wasn't supposed to be close.

And it wasn't. UNC's 103-64 victory was decided by halftime, if not long before.

Essentially, it was decided when these teams stepped onto the court at Bon Secours Wellness Arena. No. 16 seed Texas Southern, the champion of the Southwestern Athletic Conference, faced a considerable task, after all.

Since the NCAA tournament expanded to 64 teams in 1985, no No. 16 seed had ever defeated a No. 1 seed. That didn't appear likely to change on Friday, what with the Tigers' on-court deficiencies, and their lack of size — their lack of talent, relative to UNC.

They arrived in Greenville as the worst 3-point shooting team in the NCAA tournament field. They were also the worst defensive rebounding team in the tournament, and those two things — lack of shooting and an inability to rebound — doomed them from the start.

And yet Texas Southern had hope, anyway. The day before, Demontrae Jefferson, the team's 5-7 point guard, said he really believed that the impossible was possible. On the other side of the room, Zach Lofton, the SWAC Player of the Year, spoke with confidence about his team's chances.

And then the game began, and the stark differences between these teams became clearer. One was obvious enough just by sight: UNC (28-7) wore its usual home white uniforms, some of the most iconic in college basketball, adorned with the Nike "Jump Man" logo near the chest.

Texas Southern (23-12), meanwhile, wore jerseys made by Russell Athletic. They wouldn't have been out of place had they been found hanging in a locker inside an old Texas YMCA. Another difference: Texas Southern's radio broadcast crew consisted of one man, calling the game by himself.

Nate Britt drives to the basket against Texas Southern's Stephan Bennett (15) and Zach Lofton (2). Britt finished with 10 points off the bench in North Carolina's dominating win. (Robert Willett - rwillett@newsobserver.com)

Seven seconds after it started, UNC, which advanced to play against No. 8 seed Arkansas in the second round led after Isaiah Hicks scored on an easy layup. It was an omen, indeed, for most things came easily for the Tar Heels, especially after the competitive portion of the game ended.

It lasted only about 3½ minutes. From there, after Texas Southern had valiantly tied the score at 10, UNC went on a 20-4 run during the next six minutes. Again the Tigers, hopeful as they were, admirably cut their deficit to nine points, but the Tar Heels closed the first half on a 21-5 run.

In the second half UNC's margin was never narrower than 26 points. Outside the victory the good news, for the Tar Heels, was that Justin Jackson, the junior forward who earned ACC Player of the Year honors, broke out of his recent shooting funk.

Jackson entered the NCAA tournament having missed 40 of his past 60 attempts from the field. By halftime, he'd scored 19 of his 21 points, and made all five of his 3-pointers. It was, perhaps, the sort of performance he needed to rid himself whatever had ailed him in UNC's past four games.

Jackson was one of five UNC players who scored in double-figures. Hicks finished with 17, and Kennedy Meeks 13. UNC made 51 percent of its shots and held Texas Southern to 36.7 percent shooting — a positive sign for the Tar Heels, who are seeking greater defensive consistency.

Jackson and UNC's other starters watched the final six minutes from the bench. Their work was done. UNC coach Roy Williams, preparing his team for the grind of the NCAA tournament, went deep into his bench, and did so early.

Nine UNC players received at least 10 minutes of playing time. Nobody among them played for more than 24 minutes. UNC coach Roy Williams emptied his bench, and called for the walk-ons, with a little less than four minutes remaining.

Moments later, Kanler Coker, a senior guard who plays sparingly, scored the Tar Heels' 101st point on a reverse layup that had his teammates looking up at the video board to see a replay. By then the result had been long decided. The Ocean of Soul played on, belting out a loud, brassy tune, while the Tar Heels marched on. ■

Justin Jackson fires up a 3-pointer in the first half against Texas Southern. Jackson had a terrific game with 21 points, seven rebounds and three assists. (Chuck Liddy - cliddy@newsobserver.com)

UNC players (left to right) Kenny Williams (suit), Theo Pinson (1),
Justin Jackson (44) and Nate Britt (0) react after little-used reserve
Kanler Coker scores near game's end against Texas Southern.
(Chuck Liddy - cliddy@newsobserver.com)

MARCH 19, 2017 · GREENVILLE, SOUTH CAROLINA
NORTH CAROLINA 72, ARKANSAS 65

SWEET COMEBACK

UNC Rallies Late, Defeats Arkansas to Advance to Sweet 16

By Andrew Carter

North Carolina stared the end of its season in the face on Sunday — the end of so many dreams and hopes, and the end of a long pursuit of redemption that has driven this team for nearly a year now — and the Tar Heels didn't blink.

They trailed Arkansas by five points with 3½ minutes to play and then, in those tense moments of prolonged futility and dying dreams, UNC's situation appeared bleak, indeed. The Tar Heels had already lost a 17-point lead. They had lost their ability to run their offense.

They had lost their composure, in moments, and now they were 3½ minutes away from losing their season, and the goal of avenging one of the most heartbreaking defeats in NCAA tournament history. Just when it appeared at its most lost, though, UNC found a way. Somehow.

The Tar Heels scored the final 12 points, and Justin Jackson's authoritative dunk in the final seconds provided a signature moment in UNC's 72-65 victory. And with that, UNC is onto a regional semifinal for the 35th time in school history.

Top-seeded UNC advanced to the South Regional semifinals, where it will play against Butler, the No. 4 seed. There will be time to digest that match-up, and analyze it. In the meantime, it might take a while to figure out how the Tar Heels ever found their way against Arkansas.

"I don't mind saying I feel a little lucky," UNC coach Roy Williams said when it ended.

Arkansas' 65-60 lead with 3½ minutes remaining seemed larger than the five-point margin indicated. It seemed larger because the Razorbacks took that lead moments after a UNC turnover — one of the 10 the Tar Heels committed in the second half.

UNC then seemed doomed. It had been a second half of turnovers and missed shots and, on the other end, Arkansas at times scored in improbable ways — with the shot clock running down or, at times, with a defender in position to disrupt.

With a little less than three minutes remaining, though, Joel Berry, the junior point guard who played through ankle pain, made a pair of free throws to cut UNC's deficit to two points. The Tar Heels forced a defensive stop and then Isaiah Hicks maneuvered past the Razorbacks' defense for a dunk.

Now it was a one-point game, Arkansas leading 65-64, with two minutes, 16 seconds remaining.

"I just told my teammates to believe, and believe that we were going to win the game," said Berry, whom Williams described afterward as a "little rascal." "That's

Joel Berry II drives against Arkansas' Moses Kinglsey during UNC's dramatic victory over the Razorbacks. Nursing a sore ankle, Berry had 10 points on only two for 13 shooting from the floor. (Robert Willett - rwillett@newsobserver.com)

why I got it tattooed on the inside of my arm, that's what you gotta do is believe."

And so the Tar Heels, who reached the national championship game a season ago and lost at the buzzer against Villanova, believed. They also played some of their best defense of the season during the final few minutes.

After another defensive stop, Hicks made two free throws to give UNC the lead again, and after defensive stop Kennedy Meeks tipped in a miss, and after another defensive stop Hicks made two more free throws.

Jackson's dunk followed UNC's final defensive stop. And then it was over: UNC's 12-0 run, and the game.

"The last seven possessions we scored six times," Williams said. "The last seven possessions they didn't score. So that's some toughness there, too. I'll still say I feel lucky. But you know what? Luck is — what's that old saying — preparation meets opportunity. And the guys stepped up and made some plays too."

UNC shot only 38 percent. The Tar Heels committed 17 turnovers — 10 of them in the second half, when UNC at times appeared unnerved and out of sorts. And Berry and Justin Jackson, UNC's two leading scorers, labored through arguably their worst combined game of the season.

They missed 20 of their 27 attempts from the field, and combined for 25 points. Just when the game began to feel out of reach, though, given UNC's second-half ineptitude, the Tar Heels discovered their defensive will and managed a way to score, finally.

Six of their final 12 points came at the free-throw line. Hicks' dunk and Meeks' putback accounted for four more, and then there was Jackson's breakaway dunk in the closing seconds. After he landed he screamed, and seconds later the Tar Heels celebrated a dramatic comeback. ▪

Kennedy Meeks tips in a miss in a key moment late in the game against Arkansas. Meeks had a standout performance with 16 points and 11 rebounds. (Robert Willett - rwillett@newsobserver.com)

Justin Jackson reacts after an emphatic dunk to seal the comeback win over Arkansas. Jackson had 15 points, eight rebounds, five assists and five steals in the victory. (Robert Willett - rwillett@newsobserver.com)

MARCH 24, 2017 • MEMPHIS, TENNESSEE

NORTH CAROLINA 92, BUTLER 80

ELITE PERFORMANCE

UNC Continues Quest for Redemption with Win Over Butler

By Andrew Carter

Approaching late March, well down the way on the road to the Final Four, North Carolina on Friday night against Butler played every bit like a team driven by its season-long quest for redemption, and one worthy enough to complete the mission.

The Tar Heels, so driven to avenge a last-second loss in the national title game a year ago, might have been fortunate simply to be here, after its escape act against Arkansas. After that comeback, some UNC players said they'd never been more anxious, more nervous, than they were in the final minutes.

On Friday, though, they could relax in the final minutes of a 92-80 victory against Butler in an NCAA tournament South Regional semifinal. The drama, so thick in the final moments on against Arkansas, had long disappeared from FedEx Forum, where the Tar Heels punished the Bulldogs on both ends.

UNC, the top seed in the South Region, advanced to a regional final for the second consecutive season, and for the 27th time in school history. The Tar Heels will play either No. 2 seed Kentucky or No. 3 UCLA on Sunday, with a trip to the Final Four at stake.

This was UNC (30-7), the top seed in the South Region, at its most complete. The Tar Heels, who led 52-36 at halftime, thoroughly dominated, and did so against a quality opponent in a way they hadn't, perhaps, since the beginning of the season.

Back then, back when the Tar Heels ran past the field in the Maui Invitational in November, they did so with enough ease to suggest that, somehow, they might be even more formidable than they were last year, before losing Marcus Paige and Brice Johnson. Since, UNC had often searched to recapture its early-season form.

For long stretches on Friday night, they appeared to have found it. The Tar Heels, who shot so poorly against Arkansas, scored on 19 of their first 25 possessions, and they made 13 of their first 18 attempts from the field, and shot 54 percent.

They led 22-12 less than eight minutes in, and 30-14 about midway through the first half. That was after UNC seized control with a 20-5 run over the span of about five minutes. Joel Berry, the junior point guard, scored half of UNC's points during that run.

Entering Friday, Berry had been the subject of much scrutiny and many questions, most of them about his right ankle — he called those "annoying" on Thursday — and others about his shooting. He'd missed 11 of his 13 shot attempts against Arkansas, after all, and played through ankle pain.

Berry said he felt good on Thursday. His performance supported it.

Joel Berry II attacks the basket against Butler's Tyler Lewis (1) in North Carolina's 92-80 win. Berry had a huge game with 26 points. (Robert Willett - rwillett@newsobserver.com)

He finished with a team-high 26 points, while Justin Jackson, the junior wing forward who earned ACC Player of the Year honors, finished with 24. That was one of the main differences between Sunday and Friday.

Against Arkansas, Berry and Jackson missed 20 of their 27 attempts from the field. Against Butler, they made 17 of their 31 shots, and they combined to make five 3-pointers. By halftime, they'd scored a combined 27 points, two more than they scored in 40 minutes on Sunday.

Jackson and Berry were only but a part of the story for UNC during the first half. Luke Maye, the sophomore forward, played a starring role, too.

Maye has become an important role player. Roy Williams, the UNC coach, appreciates his hustle, his knack for rebounding, his ability to keep possessions alive with his grit. Maye provided more than those admirable characteristics against Butler.

By halftime he'd scored 14 points, a college high, and he'd made three 3-pointers. He finished with 16 points and 12 rebounds, his first double-double. Maye's third 3-pointer, which bounced off the front of the rim before falling in, provided a sign that maybe this was UNC's night.

Still, the Tar Heels had to work. The Bulldogs, who shot 44 percent against UNC's aggressive defense, cut its deficit, as large as 20 points, to 10 points with six minutes remaining, and to 11 with about 3½ minutes to play. Each time, though, UNC responded, and its lead never shrunk into single digits.

In the final minutes on Sunday, UNC's reserves sat nervously on the bench, the specter of a season-ending defeat driving their anxiety. In the final minutes on Friday, some of them entered the game. Williams emptied his bench with 45 seconds remaining. The Tar Heels' march continued. ∎

Butler's Tyler Wideman is called for the offensive foul as he runs into North Carolina's Isaiah Hicks the second half of UNC's Sweet 16 win. (Ethan Hyman - ehyman@newsobserver.com)

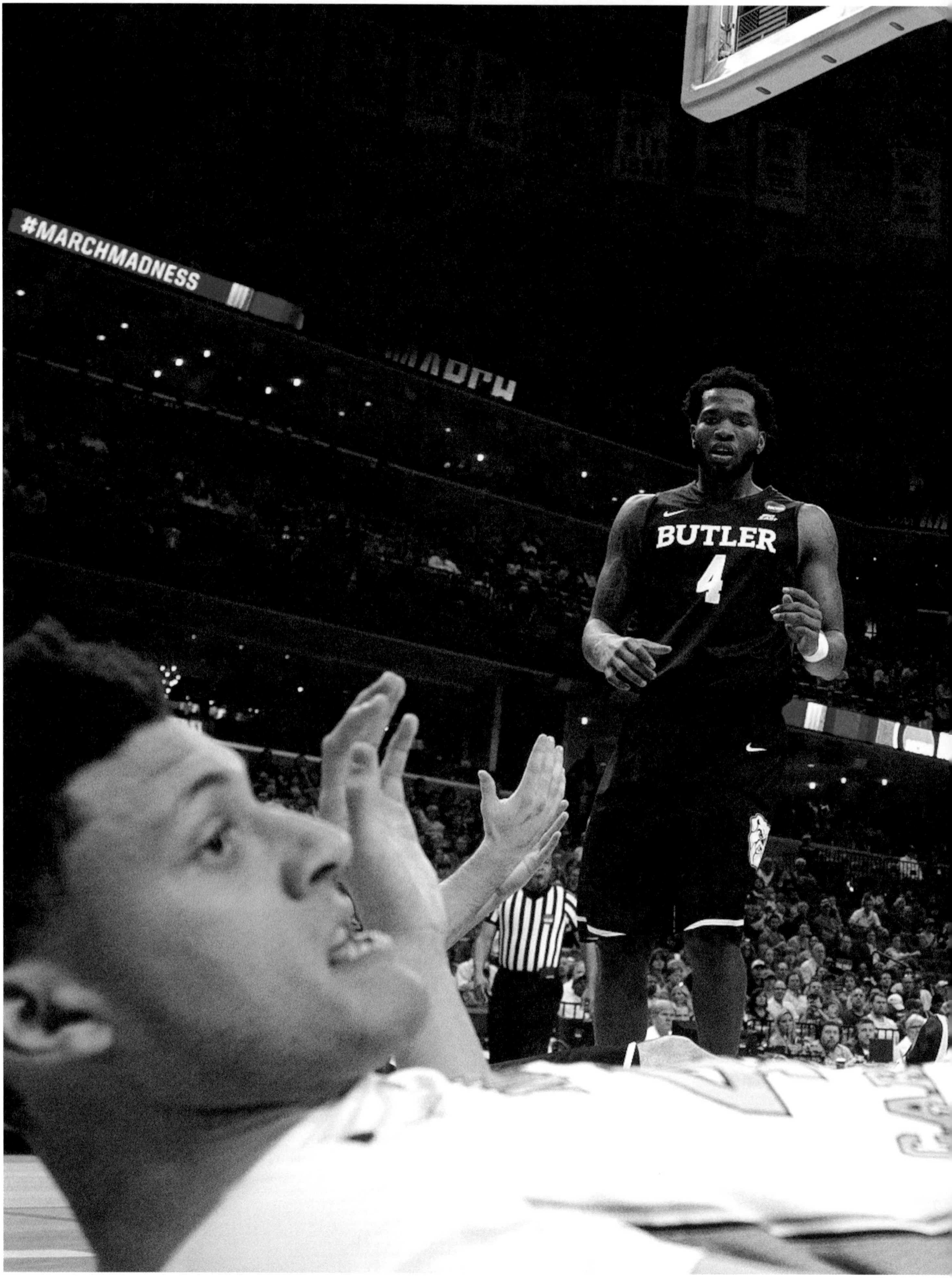
#MARCHMADNESS
BUTLER
4

Justin Jackson looks to the officials for a foul call after falling to the court during the first half against Butler. Jackson continued his exemplary play during the NCAA Tournament, with 24 points, five rebounds and five assists. (Robert Willett - rwillett@newsobserver.com)

MAYE DAY

Luke Maye's Shot Gives UNC Win Over Kentucky, Last Spot in Final Four

By Andrew Carter

From Murphy to Manteo and all parts in between, children in North Carolina will go to their driveways in the weeks and years to come and they'll stand to the left of the basket, a tie game in their imaginations, and they'll try to recreate what Luke Maye did on Sunday.

From Murphy to Manteo, they'll be talking about North Carolina's 75-73 victory against Kentucky in the South Regional championship game for a long, long time to come — maybe for as long as the Tar Heels ever play basketball.

They'll talk about a game that had a little bit of everything — floor slaps and screams, momentum swings and monumental shots, none of them more important than the one Maye, the Tar Heels sophomore reserve turned March hero, forever, made inside of the final second, his team's season hanging in the balance.

Moments after Kentucky's Malik Monk improbably tied the score at 73 with a long, contested 3-pointer, Maye, the Tar Heels' sophomore forward, made the shot of his life: a jumper from the left side, just inside the 3-point line, with three-tenths of a second left.

"I just kind of stepped back and he gave me the ball," Maye said, "and I just shot it. And luckily it went in. It was a great feeling."

The officials took a look at it, just to see whether it was a 3-pointer or a two. After determining that Maye was inside the line, Kentucky (32-6) had three-tenths of a second left. But the Wildcats' in-bounds pass sailed the length of the court and went out of bounds.

Seconds later, UNC's celebration began. The victory sends the Tar Heels, the top seed in the South Region, to the Final Four for the 20th time. They will play against Oregon, which emerged from the Midwest Region with a victory against Kansas, in a national semifinal in Glendale, Ariz.

Maye, who was so instrumental in UNC's 92-80 victory against Butler in the regional semifinal, again played a starring role. He finished with 17 points in 20 minutes off the bench, and he made six of his nine attempts from the field.

In back-to-back games Maye scored more points in college than he ever had before. Entering the South Regional semifinals, Maye had never scored more than 13 points in a college game. He scored 16 against Butler and then 17 on in the win over Kentucky.

The final two are the ones everyone will remember — the shot that will be replayed over and over, and reenacted in parks and playgrounds and driveways for weeks and months and maybe years to come. Maye's last-

North Carolina's newest hero Luke Maye cuts down the net following the Tar Heels' unforgettable 75-73 victory over Kentucky. (Robert Willett - rwillett@newsobserver.com)

second shot was just a part of it, though.

The Tar Heels (31-7) trailed by five points with five minutes to play, and UNC coach Roy Williams then called a timeout. Not long ago, he said he'd only call those when he dislikes the look on his players' faces, and he didn't like their expressions when Kentucky led 64-59 with about five minutes remaining.

From there UNC scored 12 consecutive points. Theo Pinson, a junior forward, made four free throws during that stretch, and Joel Berry II, a junior guard, made an important driving shot off the backboard. Berry, hobbled throughout, played through ankle pain and finished with 11 points.

UNC's lead grew as large as seven with 54 seconds to play. By then it looked like the Tar Heels might escape in comfort. Not a chance, though.

Kentucky's De'Aaron Fox made a 3-pointer to cut UNC's lead to four, and Monk, who scored 47 points against UNC the first time these teams played, back in Kentucky's 103-100 victory on Dec. 17 in Las Vegas, made a 3-pointer of his own to cut Kentucky's deficit to 71-70 with 39 seconds remaining.

Junior forward Justin Jackson, who led UNC with 19 points, made a layup on the other end to give the Tar Heels

Opposite: Luke Maye releases the game winning shot, two of his 17 points in the win. Above: Maye reacts after hitting the clutch shot, sure to go down among the most memorable shots in UNC history. (Ethan Hyman - ehyman@newsobserver.com)

a three-point lead with 34 seconds remaining. And that set up Monk, again. His 3-pointer sent the Kentucky fans into a state of delirium, and the shot tied the score at 73 with nine seconds left.

The Tar Heels didn't take a timeout then. There was no diagramming of a last-second play, no time to discuss strategy. Williams simply let his players play.

"We always say if it's more than six seconds, 'Attack,' we're going to attack, we're not going to call a time-out," Williams said. "It was 7.2, I think, when they scored and I was just screaming 'go, go, go.' And Theo goes down the court and finds Luke, and Luke made a big-time shot."

Pinson brought the ball up the court — eight seconds left, seven, six … — and soon enough Maye had it in his hands, time running out. He hesitated for a quick second and then jumped and released.

The ball rotated toward the basket for a couple of moments as the FedEx Forum was quiet, almost silent. Then the shot fell in, and they'll be talking about it for a long, long time to come. ◼

Opposite: Kennedy Meeks, Nate Britt (0) and Isaiah Hicks accept the South Regional championship trophy following their 75-73 victory over Kentucky. Above: Roy Williams celebrates the ninth trip to the Final Four in his coaching career. (Robert Willett - rwillett@newsobserver.com)

The Tar Heels advanced to the Final Four
for the 20th time in program history.
(Robert Willett - rwillett@newsobserver.com)